TOURISM, MUSEUMS AND THE LOCAL ECONOMY

Tourism, Museums and the Local Economy

The Economic Impact of the
North of England Open Air Museum at Beamish

Peter Johnson and Barry Thomas
University of Durham

Edward Elgar

Published by
Edward Elgar Publishing Limited
Gower House
Croft Road
Aldershot
Hants GU11 3HR
England

Edward Elgar Publishing Limited
Distributed in the United States by
Ashgate Publishing Company
Old Post Road
Brookfield
Vermont 05036
USA

A CIP catalogue record for this book is available from the British Library

Library of Congress Cataloging-in-Publication Data

Johnson, Peter, 1944–
    Tourism, museums and the local economy: the economic impact of the North of England Open Air Museum at Beamish/Peter Johnson and Barry Thomas.
      p. cm.
    Includes bibliographical references.
    1. North of England Open Air Museum. 2. Tourist trade—Economic aspects—England—Stanley Region (Derwentside) I. Thomas, R. Barry. II. Title.
AM101,S558J64 1992
942.2'7'0074—dc20

91–42104
CIP

ISBN 1 85278 617 5

Printed and bound in Great Britain by
Billing and Sons Ltd, Worcester

Contents

Figures

Tables

Preface

This book draws together the fruits of a programme of research work which has ranged over many aspects of the study of the economic impact of tourist attractions. Its central focus is on Beamish Museum.

It is hoped that the main concern of the present volume – providing a framework for assessing economic impact, and measurement of this impact in the case of Beamish – will be of interest to a broad group of readers. These include economists and geographers (particularly those with an interest in tourism, the arts and museums, and regional development), and professionals and others involved in museum or tourism management, administration and research. Policymakers in central and local government may also find the study of value. Much of the book is written in a style which should be intelligible to all these readers, though in certain parts the argument is technical and may not be readily understood by readers unfamiliar with economic analysis. The two chapters which contain technical material are those on the employment impact (Chapter 4, especially Sections 4.2.2 and 4.3) and on visitor demand (Chapter 5, especially Section 5.4). These passages can be skipped by those readers who do not wish to examine the formal economics: non-technical introductions and summaries are provided in these chapters.

A number of the ideas and results presented in this book have appeared, often in a preliminary form, in a series of discussion papers. There have also been several journal articles and contributions to books which have contained early versions of some of the work. Some of this published material has been used as a starting point in writing parts of the present volume. The authors are grateful for permission to use material which originally appeared in: Chris Cooper (ed.) *Progress in Tourism, Recreation and Hospitality Management*, Vol. 3, Belhaven Press, 1991; Gaynor Kavanagh (ed.) *The Museums Profession*, Leicester University Press, 1991; *Museum Management and Curatorship*; *Regional Studies*; *Tourism Management*; and the *Northern Economic Review*.

The research on which this book is based was financed by the Joseph Rowntree Foundation, which has also financially supported its publication. The Foundation's generous assistance is gratefully acknowledged. Dr Janet Lewis, Research Director of the Foundation provided all the help and encouragement that we needed.

The research would not have been possible without the active support of Peter Lewis, the Director of Beamish Museum, and his staff. John Gall, Deputy Director, Peter Blagden, Marketing Director and Rosemary Allan, Senior Keeper in Social History, were all extremely helpful, as were a number of other staff. Frank Atkinson, the first Director of the Museum, also kindly discussed the project with us. Peter Lewis, along with Professor S.R.C. Wanhill of Surrey University, Alan Townsend of the University of Durham's Geography Department, and Michael Reece, sometime Director of the Northumbria Tourist Board, served on the advisory committee for this research. Colleagues in the Department of Economics at the University of Durham were most supportive and provided a useful sounding board for ideas. John Ashworth and Adrian Darnell both worked very productively and helpfully on specific aspects of the project. Dave Byrne of the Department of Sociology and Social Policy at Durham provided unstinting expert advice on our survey work. Ruth Towse of the University of Exeter kindly read a draft of the manuscript and made some valuable suggestions for improvement which have been incorporated into the final version. In addition, seminar audiences at the Universities of Leicester and Durham offered helpful comments.

During the course of this research the authors had discussions with management in open air museums in the United Kingdom, the Netherlands, Scandinavia and the USA. The patient willingness of busy museum directors and their staff to discuss – often over several hours, or in one case, days – the economic effect of their museums was most welcome.

Secretarial support was supplied most efficiently by Julie Bushby and Lovaine Ord.

The help of all of these people has been much appreciated. None however bears any responsibility for any errors or omissions.

Peter Johnson and Barry Thomas,
Durham

1   The purpose of the study

1.1   Introduction

This book is concerned with evaluating the local economic impact, measured in employment terms, of a major tourist attraction in the North-East of England. This attraction is the North of England Open Air Museum at Beamish (hereafter Beamish). The following sections of this chapter set out the purpose of the book more fully, and provide some background information on the Museum.

1.2   A brief description of Beamish

Beamish Museum, which now has half a million visitors a year, opened its first (temporary) exhibition in 1971. Initial funding was provided by a consortium of local authorities, which still contributes a significant, though declining, proportion of Museum funds. The Museum occupies 300 acres in a rural area near Stanley in County Durham. Its open-air site offers a 'living' portrayal of the way of life in rural, urban and industrial areas of the North-East of England in the period immediately preceding the First World War.

The site contains numerous buildings which have been moved from all over the North-East and rebuilt using, as far as possible, the original materials. Internally, the buildings have been decorated, equipped and furnished in a style appropriate to the period depicted by the Museum. A key cluster of such buildings is the Town, officially opened in 1985. Among the buildings located along the town street are a Co-op store, over which is the Dainty Dinah Tea Room; a terrace of six houses, including a solicitor's office, a dentist's practice and family home, and a music teacher's house; a print shop and stationer's; stables; and a public house, the Sun Inn. The stables house the dray horses of Newcastle Breweries, which also operates the Inn as a going concern. The Town area includes a Victorian bandstand and a municipal park. A short distance from the Town is a railway station and yard, and a signal box.

Another cluster of buildings on the site centres on life and work in the coal industry. A series of pit cottages and their gardens provide insights into domestic life among pit communities, while the drift mine – located at Beamish long before the Museum arrived – and the colliery, with its adjacent reconstructed pit heap, enable visitors to obtain some feel for working conditions in the industry. Near to the pit cottages are the recent acquisitions of a nineteenth-century Wesleyan Methodist chapel and a school.

The Museum also portrays something of the history of North-East farming. Home Farm on the periphery of the site has been restored at its original location. Buildings taken from elsewhere in the region have been added to it in recent years. In 1990, the Museum acquired the tenancy of another farm, which it is currently developing. The Visitor Centre at the entrance to the Museum houses the Museum's shop and visitor facilities.

In addition to the buildings, the Museum has an extensive transport collection. Many of the items in this collection are fully restored and in working order. Some of the locomotives are steamed in the summer months, and trams and the (replica) bus are used to transport visitors around the site.

The emphasis throughout the site is on *working* exhibits, and on contact and interaction between visitors and Museum interpreters. The latter are located throughout the buildings. They wear period costumes, and are knowledgeable about the buildings in which they are located and the people who lived in them. They frequently carry out demonstrations (for example, baking, cheese-making and quilting) using, wherever possible, methods appropriate to the period. They also provide information and guidance for visitors. According to the Museum's present Director,[1] it is this personal interpretation of the past that distinguishes Beamish from many other Museums. At Home Farm, animals are bred and reared (many from old established breeds). The Museum also organizes numerous events, many of them held in its fairground area which contains a number of traditional attractions.

There is still much room for expansion of the open-air site. Acquisition and reconstruction of additional buildings continues, as does the development of the site itself.

A short distance from the open-air site is Beamish Hall, which houses the Museum's administration and much of its collection of primary and secondary resource material relating to the region's history. This collection covers domestic life, farming and rural life, industrial and town life and, as indicated above, transport. Special collections extend over a range of interests including animal portraits, local pottery, quilts and mats, banners and advertisements.

The Museum also has an extensive photographic archive and is building up its oral history resources.

The underlying approach to the portrayal of the past which has been adopted by Beamish raises a number of important questions. For example, are visitors presented with an historically 'authentic' experience when they enter buildings which have been moved from their original environment? Again, how far does the inevitably selective nature of the experience distort the visitor's perception of the past? There is also the question of how far a museum such as Beamish should adapt the experience it offers to appeal to its visitors, without whom it could not survive. Is there a danger that concern with what pleases the customer will generate pressures on the curatorial function that could lead (in the words of an *Annual Report* of the Welsh Folk Museum) to the provision of 'a nostalgic peep show into a largely fictitious past'?[2] Or is popularity quite consistent with scholarship? There is currently substantial debate among curators about the appropriateness or otherwise of adapting the balance of museum activities so that they more closely reflect the priorities of the market-place. This debate is in turn related to the question of whether it is appropriate to see museums primarily as tourist attractions.

It is not possible to examine these issues here. Perhaps the present Director of the Museum should have the last word. In the current *Brief Guide* to the Museum, he welcomes visitors in this way:

> It is important to understand what Beamish is *not*. We hope that you will enjoy your visit but do not imagine that Beamish is a theme park solely devoted to entertainment. This is a serious museum with large and important collections of historical objects and documents. The displays are based on detailed research and scholarship. Our prime task is to explain and educate. Many other excellent museums perform that same task but in more conventional ways. You will not at Beamish find displays in glass cases. There are few labels or information panels. We believe that such techniques would make our displays less real.

1.3 Evaluating the economic impact

The measurement and evaluation of the economic impact of attractions such as Beamish has considerable policy relevance, given the emphasis that recent government statements have placed on tourism as a source of economic regeneration and growth: see, for example, Department of Employment (1986, 1987, 1989). The encouragement of tourism has been seen as a particularly effective way of increasing employment opportunities, especially for unskilled workers and young people. As a result public funding was available for many years for tourism projects under the Development of Tourism Act 1969.[3] One condition attached to such funding was that it should generate economic benefits, particularly employment, over and above those that would otherwise be forthcoming. Given this requirement, it is not surprising to find public funding often evaluated on a cost-per-job basis.

The focus here on economic impact does not imply that other considerations are not as important, or indeed more important, in evaluating the contribution made by Beamish. The assessment criteria used will depend on who is doing the evaluation. For example, few curatorial staff at Beamish or at other museums would regard economic impact as the key yardstick against which their contribution should be measured, except perhaps where it might assist their case for raising more public funds. Instead, such criteria as the excellence of the exhibitions, success in educational activities, historical accuracy and the competence with which research, conservation and cataloguing are carried out would be considered of crucial importance.

The population at large does not see the economic impact of Beamish as a particularly relevant consideration when reaching an assessment of Beamish. The typical visitor is primarily concerned with the quality of the experience he or she receives (as he or she perceives it) and whether or not value for money has been obtained. That experience may sometimes be affected as much by the quantity and quality of the visitor facilities (for example catering, retailing and toilets) on offer, as by the technical quality of the displays. Furthermore, the history of the Museum (see Chapter 2) shows quite clearly that the primary reason for setting up Beamish was not directly economic, although on a broader perspective its establishment was seen as providing a stronger regional identity and pride in a region long affected by economic decline, and thus as enhancing that region's attractiveness to incoming industry. Early promotional literature on the Museum,[4] designed to enlist support for the project, also mentioned likely economic benefits, but such considerations were not the driving force behind the Museum's formation.[5]

It is not the purpose of this study to deny the significance of other perspectives, but whatever their validity, economic impact remains an important external yardstick for assessment which is directly relevant for policy purposes. Certainly, economic impact has been widely studied: see, for example, Henderson (1975), Vaughan (1976, 1977, 1986) and Williams *et al.* (1977).

Apart from its policy relevance, the assessment of economic impact also raises a number of interesting and significant empirical and conceptual issues which are worthy of study in their own right. In this context, it should be noted that the analytical framework used to examine the economic impact of Beamish and the questions raised by the application of that framework are not Beamish specific; they have applicability across a wide range of activities and organizations.

Economic impact may be variously interpreted. At its most comprehensive, it may be defined as the effect of Beamish on total social welfare. An all-embracing analysis of this kind would need to be very wide ranging (and expensive). It would also raise substantial problems, for example in relation to the assessment of non-quantifiable benefits. The latter may come from a variety of sources including increased regional pride, a more informed understanding, on the part of the local population and visitors to the area, of the region's past, and/or the general improvement in the quality of life which results from having a major museum nearby. Some individuals may benefit from having the *option* of visiting the museum even though they may never take up that option. (For a discussion of option demand, see Hughes, 1989). Certain costs – for example the disutility that residents may suffer as a result of congestion and noise in the vicinity, and the presence of the world's only specially constructed coal tip – also raise formidable measurement problems.

In this study, a rather more modest approach is adopted. The exclusive focus here is on the employment effects of Beamish. These effects are measured in physical rather than utility terms. (The units in which employment is measured are discussed in Chapter 4.) Although employment is clearly a narrower concern than social welfare, it nevertheless remains of considerable significance. It contributes to an area's prosperity and is complementary to other measures of economic impact, such as the effects on incomes or value added. The policy interest in employment has already been mentioned. This interest, which has spawned a number of estimates of the scale of tourism employment at the economy-wide level (Vaughan and Long, 1982; Johnson and Thomas, 1990c) and at the level of the individual project (Thiew *et al.*, 1983) or area (Barnett,

1984), is enhanced in the case of Beamish by the three factors outlined in the next section.

1.4   The significance of Beamish for employment

The first reason why Beamish is important in the context of tourism employment relates to the region in which it is located: the North of England has long been, and still is, an area of relatively high unemployment, a characteristic caused primarily by the decline of heavy industry. In the Northern Standard Region, the unemployment rate was 8.6 per cent in September 1990, compared with 5.9 per cent for the UK as a whole (*Employment Gazette*, November 1990, Table 2.4). The local authority district in which Beamish is located (Derwentside) suffered particularly badly from the contraction of the coal and steel industries in the 1970s. British Steel, the district's major employer during this decade, closed in 1980. This closure had effects on allied industries and suppliers, and although some industry has been attracted to the area, the unemployment rate has remained high in national terms. At the same time, and almost certainly as a result of economic decline, the population has been declining and is likely to continue to fall.[6] Any development of employment opportunities – particularly in a growth area such as tourism – therefore generates public interest.

Secondly, the museum is located in an area which is relatively *under-represented* in terms of tourism activity. So there may be some grounds for arguing that the potential for developing additional tourism employment is higher than elsewhere. (Whether or not more tourism employment is desirable is another matter.)

The relatively low level of tourism activity in Northumbria (Cleveland, Durham, Northumberland and Tyne and Wear) can be seen from Table 1.1, which presents some *tourism intensity* measures for the English Tourist Board regions in the first three columns. Area (square kilometres) has been used to standardize for size across Tourist Board regions. This method has obvious limitations – for example mountainous areas are likely to differ in their tourism potential from coastal areas of a similar scale – but it is probably the most appropriate measure available. The expenditure figures used in column 1 – which are derived from a survey conducted for the British Tourist Authority and the English Tourist Board – involve some estimation and should therefore be treated as indicating broad

Table 1.1 Tourism intensities by Tourist Board region

Tourist Board region	1 Estimated holiday expenditure in 1988 by British residents per square kilometre (£m)	2 Estimated holiday expenditure in 1986 by overseas residents per square kilometre (£m)	3 Number of visitors to attractions in 1988 per square kilometre (000s)	4 Overseas visitors as percentage of all visitors to attractions in 1986
Northumbria	12	2	0.71	9
Cumbria	23	3	0.46	8
N.W. England	46	7	4.66	10
Yorks. and Humberside	21	3	1.35	10
Heart of England	12	4	1.45	17
E. Midlands	13	6	1.24	7
Thames and Chilterns	13	6	1.66	22
E. Anglia	26	3	0.93	7
London	174	798	29.75	40
W. Country	52	5	1.34	13
Southern	77	6	2.42	8
S.E. England	37	14	2.35	13
England	30	14	1.87	17

Sources: *British Tourism Market, 1988*, London: British Tourist Authority/English Tourist Board Research Services, 1989.
Sightseeing in 1988, London: British Tourist Authority/English Tourist Board Research Services, 1989.
Regional Trends 23, 1988 Edition, London: HMSO, 1989.
Special tabulations for 1986 from the International Passenger Survey.

magnitudes only. They cover expenditure by British residents while away from home and on advance payments for such items as fares and accommodation. Expenditure by day trippers is excluded.

Expenditure data used in the second column are derived from special tabulations from the International Passenger Survey (IPS) prepared for the authors in 1986 (later years are not available). These data exclude transport costs and relate to expenditure by visitors from outside the United Kingdom. Because of the way in which the IPS is carried out, there may be some under-representation of regions including Northumbria, where points of entry/exit are relatively few. However, even taking this limitation into account, it would be difficult to avoid the conclusion that Northumbria receives a relatively very low level of holiday spending by overseas residents. London and the South provide an overwhelming magnet for such expenditure.

The number of visitors to attractions per square kilometre is given in column 3. This measure does not of course fully capture the pull of areas of natural beauty which, almost by definition, are under-represented in terms of conventional tourist attractions although visitor centres in (for example) national parks are included. It should also be noted that the term 'attraction' covers a wide range of buildings and activities, from theme parks to cathedrals, and regions vary in their mix of such attractions. Again the figures suggest relatively small numbers of visitors for Northumbria. The final column shows, not surprisingly, that Northumbria has a relatively low proportion of its total visitors to attractions who are from overseas.

An apparently different picture of the region is derived from Table 1.2, which shows the importance of 'tourism-related' employment in the North and in Great Britain as a whole for 1987 (the latest year for which Census of Employment data are available). Because of its exceptional position, London is excluded from the UK figures. Tourism-related employment – a category based on the Standard Industrial Classification and devised by the Department of Employment – covers a very wide spectrum of activities, not all of which are generated by tourism spending. For example, public houses and bars, and sport and recreation services draw their custom from the local population as well as from people staying away from home. Furthermore, the latter may not all be holidaymakers (Table 1.1 is

Table 1.2 Tourism-related employment, 1987

Sector	% of total number of employees in employment	
	North	United Kingdom excluding Greater London
Restaurants, snack bars, cafes and other eating places	0.8	1.1
Public houses and bars	1.6	1.3
Night clubs and licensed clubs	1.4	0.7
Hotels	1.1	1.1
Other accommodation	0.1	0.2
Libraries, museums and art galleries	0.3	0.3
Sport and other recreation services	1.7	1.4
Total, tourism-related industries	7.0	6.1

Source: Employment Gazette, October 1989.

restricted to holiday tourism). The 'North' in Table 1.2 is defined on a Standard Region basis and therefore includes Cumbria. On a straight head-count basis, the North has relatively more employees in employment in tourism-related industries than the UK, excluding London. The main explanation for this is the relatively high employment in public houses and clubs in the North. These activities tend to employ a much higher proportion of part-time staff.

It is also interesting to note that the *growth* in tourism-related employment between 1981 and 1987 was lowest in the Northern Region.[7]

The third reason why Beamish is of particular relevance for the encouragement of tourism employment is that it is a footloose development in the sense that it could have been located virtually anywhere in the North. Many museums, such as Ironbridge, by their very nature do not have such flexibility, since they must necessarily be located at a particular geographical spot; most buildings at Beamish have been brought to the site and then reconstructed in a 'typical' setting. This footloose character has obvious attractions from a policy viewpoint since it would in principle be possible to engineer the location of such an attraction in a way that maximizes employment effects.

1.5 Defining the reference area
In measuring the local employment effects of Beamish it is vitally
important to define clearly the geographical reference area that
constitutes 'the local economy'. Such a task is not straightforward.
If finance is locally provided then the benefits identifiable within the
jurisdiction of the funding authorities would seem relevant. Yet this
may not coincide with an area based on some clearer economic
rationale, such as a 'travel to work' area or a local network of
suppliers and competitors. In practice it is usually necessary to take
some area defined in administrative or political terms such as one of
the Standard Regions or a local authority area. This imposes a slight
arbitrariness on the results, because the economic impact is normally
one of diminishing geographical response rather than a sudden cut-
off at some boundary. The size of the multiplier will, of course, vary
with the size of the reference area – the smaller the area the larger the
import leakages and the smaller the multiplier – and, as shown later
in this chapter, the net employment impact may be crucially affected.

In this study the reference area is the North-East of England, that
is the counties of Durham, Northumberland, Cleveland and the 'old'
Tyne and Wear. (Throughout this volume all references to the
North-East are to these four counties.) An important consideration
in selecting this area was the fact that the constituent local authorities have been the principal source of continuing financial support
for the Museum. In some contextual material it is necessary, because
of data limitations, to use other boundaries but the main empirical
study examines only the North-East.

1.6 Beamish as a tourist attraction
Beamish is the largest tourist attraction in Northumbria (Johnson
and Thomas, 1990f). This can be seen from Table 1.3, which
provides data on major tourist attractions in the North-East. The
data must be treated cautiously, particularly where estimates are
given. It should also be noted that only clearly identifiable attractions with 100 000 or more visitors in 1989 are included in the table.
However, the leading position of Beamish in the region is clear.
Preston Hall, its nearest rival, makes no admission charge. Furthermore Beamish showed the most rapid growth in visitor numbers
between 1985 and 1989 apart from the South Shields Museum and

Table 1.3   Tourist attractions in the North-East with 100 000 or more
             visitors in 1989

Attraction	Visitor numbers			Admission charge
	1985	1989	% Change 1985/89	
Museums and art galleries				
Beamish	289 000	486 565	68	Yes
Captain Cook's Birthplace Museum	111 633	100 000[1]	−10	Yes
Laing Art Gallery, Newcastle	93 855	104 229	11	No
Preston Hall Museum, Cleveland	379 787	462 317	22	No
South Shields Museum and Art Gallery	55 000	139 558	154	No
Sunderland Museum and Art Gallery	174 111	122 550	−30	No
Historic Properties				
Bamburgh Castle	82 000	115 328	41	Yes
Durham Cathedral	341 000	400 296[1]	17	No
Housesteads Roman Fort	115 069	129 032	12	Yes

1. 1988 figure.

Source: *Tourism Fact Sheets: Northumbria* and *Sightseeing in the UK, 1989*, prepared by BTA/ETB Research Services for the four national tourism boards.

Art Gallery. (The latter recently opened its Catherine Cookson Gallery; admission to this museum is also free.)

Despite the fact that its financial and employment scale is modest relative to some of the major national museums,[8] whose collections and research activities are large in comparison, Beamish is widely recognized as an important and innovative development in the broader UK museum scene. Hudson (1987) in his influential book includes Beamish in his select world list of 37 museums which over the last two centuries have broken new ground in such an original and striking way that other museums have felt disposed or compelled to follow their example. He goes on to say that originality itself is not sufficient to justify inclusion in his list:

> It must have been significant and worthwhile originality, not mere novelty. This means that each museum, by its existence, its approach and style has met a real social need. It will have both echoed a national or international change of mood and encouraged its development. This implies of course that the influence of these pioneering institutions has been felt by the general public, their visitors and not only by other museums. (1987: vii)

Beamish was not the first open-air museum. In 1891, Skansen in Stockholm was started – in fact it grew out of an existing museum, the Nordic Museum, set up in 1873 – and this was the forerunner of all open-air museums. It was followed in 1912 by the Netherlands Open Air Museum at Arnhem. In the UK, the Welsh Folk Museum at St Fagans, near Cardiff, was established in 1949 and the Ulster Folk Museum in 1958 (see Appendix 8 and Johnson and Thomas, 1990b, for further historical details on these museums).

Yet Beamish has some claim to be innovative at least as far as the UK is concerned. Its strong commitment to industrial as well as rural history provided a new emphasis: in Hudson's words (1987: 31), the museum 'brought industrial society uncompromisingly within the definition of a folk museum'. (It is worth noting that the *original* proposal was for a museum that was primarily rural in character: see p. 16.) The sheer scale of the Beamish site also gave a new flexibility and potential to open-air operations. And on the organizational side, it was the first open-air museum to be developed by a consortium of local authorities. The significance of Beamish was given explicit recognition when it received the Museum of the Year award in 1986 and the European Museum of the Year award a year later.

1.7   The value of a case study

Despite its local and national importance, the Museum still remains only one attraction among many. The pros and cons of case studies are well known to researchers and need not be rehearsed in detail again here, but the following points are worth making.

First, the focus on the employment effects of a single attraction enables much more attention to be paid to the micro processes that generate those effects. This is particularly important when the relationships between Beamish, its supplying organizations and surrounding economic activities are analysed. Secondly, as indicated earlier, the methodology used and issues raised have direct relevance for other employment impact studies. Finally, in the last chapter of this book the experience of Beamish is compared with that of other similar museums in the UK and elsewhere.

While it is not difficult to justify the kind of study presented here, at the same time it is important to be aware of the fact that the precise unit of analysis adopted is bound to affect the interpretation of results, especially where comparisons across studies are made. This study is concerned with a single organization, but it would in principle be possible to take a group of activities such as 'museums in County Durham' or 'tourist attractions in the North-East'. If a number of projects is being considered then the extent to which they are complementary or competitive becomes important. Comparisons between the impact of a single organization and that of a group of organizations must be treated very cautiously.[9]

1.8 Other issues
The operation of a museum such as Beamish raises a wide range of issues of economic interest which are not directly related to its economic impact. For example, what precisely is the 'output' of the museum, and how should it be measured and valued? Questions such as these assume particular significance in relation to the research and scholarly activities of the museum, where public-good attributes are likely to be present. 'Outputs' such as the encouragement of a regional identity and pride and the provision of the visiting option – for present and/or future generations – also pose particular difficulties. In addition, the special nature of museum activities raises important questions about the appropriate scale of public funding (Peacock and Godfrey, 1974), many of which have been discussed in the more general context of the 'economics of the arts': see for example Robbins (1963), Throsby and Withers (1979, 1986), Hendon *et al.* (1980), Myerscough (1988), Grampp (1989), Frey and Pommerehne (1989).

The wider economic issues associated with the operation of Beamish are not treated in great depth in this study, although their importance is readily acknowledged: see Johnson and Thomas (1991b).

1.9   The structure of the book

In the next chapter, the history of the Museum since its inception in 1972 is traced, since a knowledge of the Museum's development is essential for understanding how its employment impact has built up over time. Chapter 3 examines the structure and characteristics of the Museum's labour force, and also looks at recent trends in employment. Chapter 4, the core of the study, presents the conceptual and empirical framework used to analyse the employment impact of Beamish and provides some empirical estimates of that impact. A key determinant here is the number of visitors, so the determinants of visitor demand are considered in Chapter 5. The employment potential of the Museum is analysed in Chapter 6, which also presents some of the policy implications of the study. The Appendices provide supporting material.

Notes

1. *Beamish: A Brief Guide*, published by Beamish Museum.
2. *Annual Report 1987/88*, National Museum of Wales, p. 21.
3. This funding was stopped as far as England was concerned in 1989. See Department of Employment press release, 6 July 1989.
4. For example, in one of the first public documents to promote the concept of the Museum, *Living History: An Open Air Museum for the North of England*, the values of the proposed museum in terms of the business it would generate was stressed. This document was published by the newly formed Friends of the Museum in 1968, four years before the Museum's official opening. It was largely written by Frank Atkinson, who was to become the first Director of the Museum, and was circulated to local councillors and other interested parties.
5. It is interesting to note that economic benefits, particularly employment, have sometimes figured prominently in the decision to set up or expand other museums. For example employment was an important consideration in the original discussions over the establishment of the Zuiderzee Museum in the Netherlands: see Appendix 8. At Colonial Williamsburg, in Virginia, Rockefeller authorized further building work in 1938 partly to provide useful work for young architects in Virginia during economic recession (Hudson, 1987: 148).
6. The population fell by 13 per cent between 1961 and 1986 and is expected to fall by a further 6 per cent between 1986 and 1996. See *Derwentside L.A.D. Profile*, mimeo, Training Commission, Durham Area Office (no date; probably 1988).
7. The increase in tourism-related employment was 0.3 per cent in the Northern region compared with 11.1 per cent for Great Britain as a whole. This is largely accounted for by the decline in employment in clubs (-18.4 per cent in the North compared with $+1.2$ per cent for Great Britain) and the slow growth in sports and recreation ($+0.6$ per cent in the North compared with 10.5 per cent for Great Britain). These trends offset the substantial growth in public houses and bars where the North ($+15.8$ per cent) almost matched the national average (16.1 per cent).
8. Beamish still ranks as one of the bigger museums; in 1988 there were only 20 museums in England whose visitor numbers exceeded those of Beamish. Over half these were in London, and many do not charge for admission. See *Sightsee-*

ing in 1988, Appendix A, published by the British Tourist Authority and the English Tourist Board, 1989.
9. The work by Myerscough (1988) differs from the present study in that museums are examined as part of a wider investigation into the arts as a whole.

2 The development of the Museum[1]

2.1 Introduction

The estimates of the employment impact of Beamish given in Chapter 4 relate to one year only, 1989. In interpreting these results it is important to bear in mind that this impact was not created instantly, but took many years to develop. This chapter therefore provides an historical perspective on Beamish, tracing its development from its beginnings to the present day.

Section 2.2 provides a brief outline of the Museum's history. Section 2.3 identifies factors that have played a key role in the development of the Museum and assesses the latter's success on various criteria. Section 2.4 suggests some tentative generalizations that might be made from the Museum's development.

2.2 The historical background

2.2.1 Developing the concept: November 1958 – September 1966

The first formal proposal for an open-air museum in the region was put to Durham County Council's Bowes Museum sub-committee on 27 November 1958.[2] The proposal was prepared by Frank Atkinson the (then) newly appointed Curator of Bowes Museum at Barnard Castle, whose ideas originated from a visit to an open-air museum in Scandinavia in 1952.[3] His initial proposal envisaged a museum that was primarily rural in character.[4] In February 1959, the sub-committee agreed that the existing collection at Bowes should be enlarged and that the appropriate officers should investigate the suitability of a site for the Museum.[5]

The next few years saw the Bowes Museum build up its collections in readiness for the new Museum. The collection policy adopted by Atkinson was wide ranging, a policy which he was later vigorously to defend: 'unselective' collecting 'applied both to the general content of the material – "You offer it to us and we'll collect it!" – and also to its physical size' (Atkinson, 1985). Such an open-ended policy inevitably led to resource pressures. These early years also saw a change in emphasis on the nature of the Museum. A wider vision was articulated by Atkinson in a report in 1961:

the Museum *should attempt to record* and wherever possible *portray* all aspects of rural life from the Pennines to the harbours of the North East of England. It should also attempt to record and portray the historical background of the industries of coal mining, coking, iron and steel, leadmining, quarrying, railways, textiles etc. in relation to the North East of England. (Italics in original[6])

This quotation shows the very wide geographical and industrial coverage now envisaged for the Museum. Atkinson used this report to emphasize – with almost missionary zeal – the urgency and scale of the collections that were necessary:

It is essential that collecting be carried out as quickly and as on a big a scale as possible. It is now *almost* too late; buildings, farm implements, domestic utensils are being scrapped every day, and very few remain. Customs, traditions, ways of speech are all dying out, for modern education, the radio and television are destroying these. (Italics in original)

The Museums sub-committee took the view that, given the financial implications, this comprehensive museum concept, as opposed to the original much more limited proposal for a rural museum, could not be developed by Durham alone. It proposed that the County Council should convene a meeting of local authorities with a view to establishing a *regional* industrial museum. Such a recommendation should be seen in the context of the growing emphasis by government on regional economic development and planning that occurred in the mid-1960s.[7]

This conference eventually took place in May 1966, and was attended by government officials and representatives of 13 councils and other organizations. The local authority representatives supported the establishment of the museum in principle, although a number raised questions of location and finance, two issues which were to reappear frequently in discussions. The conference decided to set up a working party to look into the possibilities. Durham County Council subsequently agreed to defer consideration of the development of its own rural museum until the working party reported.[8]

2.2.2 *Towards a regional open-air museum: October 1966 – February 1970*
The first meeting of the working party was held on 4 October 1966. Eleven local authorities were represented. The working party agreed

that the Museum should show 'every aspect of life in the past of the region, i.e. Industrial, Agricultural, Urban life and Village life'.[9] It also resolved to call the Museum the *Regional* Open Air Museum of the North of England, and to apportion the costs of the Museum among the participating local authorities on the basis of population. At the second meeting of the working party in December,[10] a short-list of possible sites was considered. Following subsequent site inspections the working party unanimously recommended Beamish Hall, near Stanley in County Durham, as the most suitable location.

Difficulties over securing agreement between the authorities surfaced from the beginning.[11] Cumberland County Council, for example, thought that its financial contribution should reflect its relatively distant location. (It did in fact later withdraw, along with the North Riding of Yorkshire.) Darlington raised the possibility of disagreement over the Museum's location and several authorities expressed reservations about the method by which expenses were to be shared. Early agreement was also made more difficult by the fact that two authorities were in the process of being reorganized.[12] The financial pressures faced by the authorities were illustrated by their response to Atkinson's request at the end of 1966 that each authority should be asked to provide in their 1967–8 financial estimates a *pro rata* contribution of £5 000 to permit the acquisition of exhibits which might become available before the Museum's establishment and whose purchase might be a matter of urgency.[13] However, of the eleven authorities involved in the working party, only five were willing to provide a contribution at that time;[14] the idea was therefore dropped.

Over a year later – in January 1968 – and after extensive negotiations between the local authorities, the working party recommended that Beamish be purchased and the Museum developed on a long-term basis. Durham County Council would acquire the Hall and then lease part of it back to the local authority consortium. It was also recommended that a joint committee representing all the participating authorities should be set up. Atkinson's own enthusiasm and vision for the proposed museum, and the publicity he stimulated was a major factor in creating support for the project.

Also in January 1968, while negotiations between the local authorities were taking place, the 'Friends' of the Museum – a voluntary organization strongly encouraged by Atkinson – was formed to give moral and practical support. This organization grew rapidly – a year after its formation it had over 300 members – and played an important role in generating interest in and momentum for the Museum. One of its earliest tasks was to produce a promotional document which was circulated to local councillors and other interested parties.[15] The Friends also offered practical help by raising finance, assisting in public displays, and dismantling, transporting, reassembling and restoring specimens. Support for the Museum even came from the Bishop of Durham, who urged readers of his diocesan *Newsletter* to become Friends.[16]

The Joint Committee met for the first time on 16 October 1968 and recommended acceptance, with minor amendments, of a draft joint agreement. (In the mean-time Beamish Hall had been purchased by Durham County Council.) The committee also recommended starting the Museum on a 'care and maintenance' basis with an annual expenditure limited to £12 800 and a staff initially limited to three. (Atkinson had argued for a much larger initial scale.)

The next year was occupied with preliminary planning and with negotiations between the local authorities, many of whom continued to express concern over the apparently open-ended nature of their commitment.[17] This opposition was largely overcome by provision for a five-year rolling programme of development and expenditure; under this the constituent authorities would, each year, approve the programme for the following five years. Thus the authorities would be committed up to the agreed planned level of expenditure – thereby giving the Joint Committee some certainty – but they would play a crucial part in determining that level of expenditure. The agreement was finally signed by eight authorities[18] – Sunderland having dropped out owing to finance pressures – in February 1970, the month in which the first staff were employed. Atkinson was appointed first Director of the Museum.

2.2.3 *Preparations for opening: March 1970 – March 1972*
It had originally been intended to open the Museum in July 1970, but it soon became clear that this target was not attainable. In September 1970 it was proposed that a preliminary exhibition should be opened just before Whitsuntide 1971.[19]

The financial sensitivity of the participating local authorities remained clearly visible. For example, Northumberland County Council asked, in October 1970, for the estimate for net expenditure in 1971–2 to be reduced from £45 500 to £35 000 on account of economic pressures.[20] The Director and Treasurer had initially proposed an *increase* (to £52 600) to reflect, *inter alia*, the fact that the Museum would be opened in 1972 and the urgent need for new storage facilities.[21] The latter were stretched to capacity because of Atkinson's catholic collecting policy, combined with the fact that many exhibits, such as rolling stock, were very large. The Joint Committee eventually agreed to reduce the 1971–2 figure to £35 200.

The Museum's first Development Plan, written by Atkinson and the Chief Planning Officer for County Durham, was adopted in December 1970.[22] This confirmed that the objectives of the Museum were

> to study, collect, preserve and exhibit buildings, machinery, objects and information, illustrating the historical development of industry and the way of life of the North of England . . . [to] endeavour to deal comprehensively with the social, industrial and agricultural history of the region, and to bring together the buildings and artefacts of recent centuries . . ..

The resource implications of pursuing such an all-embracing set of objectives were huge and unrealistic in the light of the constraints on local authority financing which had already surfaced. The aims contained in the plan are in marked contrast to the current objective being pursued by the Museum – at least as far as its public displays are concerned – of focusing on a fairly narrowly defined pre-First World War period.[23] However, Atkinson and his supporters had little to lose in pitching the initial bid at a high level.

The first few months of 1971 saw continued intense activity in preparation for the opening of the preliminary exhibition. This exhibition, 'Museum in the Making', stayed open for 21 weekends, attracting in all about 50 000 visitors. Atkinson was quick to contrast the success of the exhibition with the very small resource base on which he was operating. He pointed out that voluntary labour, which had played a key role in mounting the exhibition, could not be relied on indefinitely, a view which received the strong support of the Chairman of the Friends.[24] He also reminded the committee that much essential museum work – for example conservation, cataloguing and research – had not been undertaken. In addition, the exhibition had experienced substantial overcrowding in peak periods. Against this background Atkinson argued for more resources, a request which the Joint Committee approved,[25] but which was later

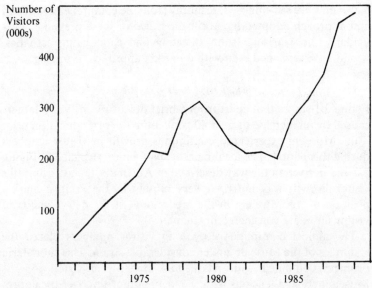

Number of
Visitors
(000s)

Source: Beamish records.

Figure 2.1 Visitor Numbers, 1971–89

turned down by the constituent authorities.[26] At the end of 1971,[27] Atkinson suggested that the idea of setting up a Trust for the Museum should be explored, a proposal that many years later reached fruition. The official opening of the Museum, based on the theme of 'Beamish Coming to Life', took place in May 1972. Again, the Museum experienced lengthy queues at peak times and severe overcrowding.[28] In all, about 80 000 visitors were attracted in 1972 (Figure 2.1).

One way to alleviate these pressures would have been through higher prices. Given the novelty value of the Museum and its very wide support among the general public, it is likely that revenue could have been increased by such a policy. However, a policy of charging what the market would bear was not appealing to the Joint Committee. Furthermore the notion of charging a substantial entry fee was alien to most public sector museums in the early 1970s. It was particularly alien to the concept of Beamish whose collections – in the words of Atkinson (1985) – were 'of the people, by the people, for the people'. To an extent the pressures experienced at the

Museum were self-imposed, resulting from the comprehensive vision and approach adopted by Atkinson. Some of these pressures, particularly those arising from collecting and cataloguing activities, would have remained even with a market approach to pricing.

2.2.4   Rapid growth: April 1972 – March 1980

Figure 2.1 shows that apart from a brief downturn in 1977 – largely caused by an increase of over 40 per cent in the real admission price – the Museum experienced continuous growth in visitor numbers during this period. The local market share index, depicted in Figure 2.2 and derived in the way described in Appendix 1, shows that this visitor growth was mirrored very closely in the *relative* market position of the Museum in the area. Some of the determinants of visitor flows are considered in Chapter 5.

The almost continuous growth in visitor numbers placed the resources of the Museum under considerable strain. This short-term problem combined with Atkinson's longer-term vision for the Museum created tensions with the local authorities over the appro-

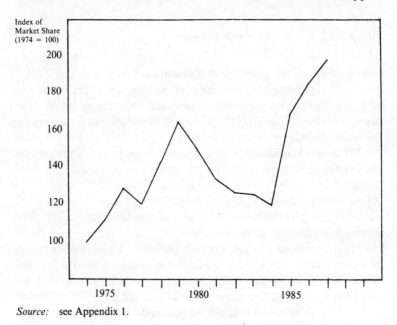

Source: see Appendix 1.

Figure 2.2   Local market share index (1974 = 100)

priate level of funding. These tensions were well illustrated in 1972, when Atkinson and the Treasurer submitted revenue expenditure estimates for 1973–4 that were more than double (at £98 500) the likely out-turn for 1972–3 and the 1973–4 figures previously agreed as part of the rolling plan.[29] The main increase in costs concerned staffing: 19 new staff were proposed. The proposed departure from the agreed rolling programme evoked a strong negative response from some constituent authorities. The Joint Committee finally agreed at its meeting in October 1972 to recommend revision of the 1973–4 estimate to approximately £80 000. This figure was later reduced to £60 800,[30] although it was also agreed that should Sunderland and Tynemouth become members, the committee should be allowed to spend any additional funds forthcoming from these authorities.

The capital programme also faced similar problems. For example in March 1973, the Joint Committee was informed that the proposed programme for 1973–4 of £80 000 was under threat. Four of the nine constituent authorities, who together contributed 53 per cent of the total capital budget, indicated that they would be unable to provide funds for that year.[31] (A fifth authority was only willing to make an allocation if all the other authorities did likewise.) Eventually, three of the four authorities who had withdrawn from capital financing relented, enabling £75 000 – much less in real terms than the 1972–3 figure – to be spent in 1973–4. One outcome of the wrangling over capital finance was the reinstitution of a rolling programme for capital development, which was seen as enabling local authorities to plan more effectively and to be aware of their commitment. But such a programme did not make commitment of funds by the local authorities any easier: even though the Joint Committee recommended that a five-year capital plan be adopted,[32] the Director's report to the Joint Committee in March 1974 recorded that the amount of capital available for 1974–5 had still not been agreed. It also added that 'the inability to maintain a steady forward planning operation makes for inefficient operation and unsatisfactory arrangements for our visitors'.[33]

Similar difficulties arose in July 1974 when the Director, at the request of the Joint Committee, submitted a development programme for the years 1974–5 to 1979–80. Characteristically, the Director took the opportunity to reiterate the crucial importance of increased revenue and capital spending if the Museum was to achieve its original aims; he proposed a very substantial increase in capital spending and in the local authority contribution. The suggested increase was too great for the Joint Committee,[34] who were clearly unable to match the Director's enthusiasm for development. The Committee proposed acceptance of a modified capital programme,[35] but a month later reported that, given the general economic crisis, the constituent authorities were able only to maintain their present commitment, possibly supplemented by support from individual authorities for particular projects. Indeed the initial budget for 1975–6 made no provision for capital development. In the event, the capital position eased as the year progressed; a particularly significant development was a grant from the English Tourist Board (ETB), which had identified Beamish as having substantial development potential. This development, though encouraging, did not ease the planning difficulties surrounding the capital programme. In view of the problems associated with local authority financing, proposals were made from a variety of sources to put the Museum on a more independent footing. For example in January 1973 the Chairman of the Friends raised the possibility that local authority financing might be linked with industrial money, with the Museum being run on a commercial basis. It was agreed that such a proposition should be 'borne in mind', a formula for deferring action. Although this option came to assume increasing importance in later discussions, practical steps in this direction were a long way off.

Then in 1976 the Joint Committee commissioned independent consultants to consider the possibility of an appeal. The consultants' report, which was submitted early in 1977, was the first *outside* assessment of the Museum and thus carried particular weight. It reiterated the financial and planning limitations that derived from local authority financing, while at the same time taking the view that the Museum was at a critical 'take off' stage. It concluded that the Museum was in some danger of outgrowing its strength, with the growth in visitor numbers placing heavy strains on facilities and management structure. As the Museum's subsequent history showed, this warning had considerable substance. The report also came out against wholesale reliance in the future on local authority financing, but added that Beamish was not yet geared up to alternative sources of income on the scale required.

Following consideration of the report, the Joint Committee

accepted the principle of an appeal.[36] It also reached agreement – short lived as it turned out – that the constituent authorities should maintain at least their present revenue contributions to Beamish, increasing them in line with inflation, with the Joint Committee seeking additional support only in exceptional circumstances. On the capital front, the Joint Committee decided to ask the constituent authorities whether they could commit themselves to a capital contribution over a period of years. In the event none was able to do so.

The appeal was formally launched in January 1979 under the aegis of a new Development Trust. Like the ETB grant, the appeal provided a source of funds independent of the constituent authorities, and complemented the greater freedom provided by those authorities when they agreed the principle of allowing the Joint Committee to keep any revenue surpluses. Another source of greater freedom for manoeuvre over capital spending came from increased assistance from outside sources of funds. An important development in this respect occurred in November 1978, when the ETB offered £200 000 towards several specified projects. The offer of this grant was conditional on a number of requirements, which were later to present major problems for the Museum. However, it marked a further important stage in the Museum's financial development. Earlier grants had been obtained from a variety of sources – including the ETB – but none had been on such a substantial scale and none had been of a *programme* nature.

On the revenue side, the growth in income from visitors meant that reliance on local authority finance declined almost continuously throughout the 1970s, as Table 2.1 shows. (The table also shows that the real value of the local authorities' revenue contribution fell between 1974–5 and 1978–9.) The Museum benefited during this period from the funding of posts by the Manpower Services Commission (MSC). At their peak, the MSC funds led to 120 extra employees at Beamish. This additional source of labour enabled a range of extra activities to be undertaken, including the improvement of storage facilities, cataloguing and the provision of information leaflets.

The increase in visitor numbers during the 1970s not only highlighted the problems of financing the Museum's growing needs from local authority sources, it also led to strains on its organization and management. The first of these surfaced in late 1979, when an internal audit of the Museum revealed a number of shortcomings in

Table 2.1 Local authorities' revenue contribution to Beamish

Financial year	% of total income of Beamish	Index of real value of contribution[1] (1971–2 = 100)	Financial year	% of total income of Beamish	Index of real value of contribution[1] (1971–2 = 100)
1970–1	n.a.	n.a.	1980–1	36.5	164.2
1971–2	84.6	100.0	1981–2	45.3	204.4
1972–3	78.1	126.0	1982–3	45.4	179.4
1973–4	77.1	182.0	1983–4	43.0	178.4
1974–5	71.5	219.7	1984–5	43.5	169.6
1975–6	68.2	198.8	1985–6	31.1	169.0
1976–7	63.3	174.8	1986–7	33.0	173.2
1977–8	52.4	148.0	1987–8	23.2	172.4
1978–9	40.0	134.9	1988–9	17.9	169.6
1979–80	42.3	182.6	1989–90	n.a.	n.a.

1. The current prices local authority contribution was deflated by the GDP deflator based on expenditure data at factor cost (see *Economic Trends, Annual Supplement 1990 Edition.* London: HMSO, 1990, Table 1).

internal procedures relating to contracts.[37] Personnel had been appointed to posts for which there was no budgetary provision and for which there had been no committee approval. As a result of this over-commitment the Museum was facing its first revenue deficit for a number of years. The problems over the deficit were compounded by the pressures local authorities were facing from central government to cut back on expenditure and by the constituent authorities' decision to charge the Museum for the administrative and other services they provided.[38]

2.2.5 The downward slide, April 1980 – March 1985

Towards the middle of 1980 the Treasurer produced a detailed document on the financial state of the Museum.[39] It made depressing reading. A number of capital projects started in previous years were either overspent or uncompleted or both, owing to 'inadequate planning and control of capital projects'. The slippage on the capital programme meant that some of the conditions attached to the ETB's £200 000 grant had not been met. As a result new terms involving a much smaller grant were eventually imposed.[40]

A further report by the Treasurer highlighted the lack of skilled manpower to design, implement and monitor the capital programme.[41] It also drew attention to the problems faced by the Museum in the short term in reacting quickly to a shortfall in its capital resources, when the Joint Committee was dependent on sources of finance over which it exercised no real control – those from the constituent authorities. The difficulties were compounded by the fact that the ETB had set current price limits on its grant, a fact not realized by the Museum, and by the assumption – incorrect as it turned out – that the local authorities would maintain their contributions constant in real terms.

A further problem emerged during the course of 1980. As Figure 2.1 shows, the number of visitors to the Museum declined significantly during this year. The Museum's local market share also declined (Figure 2.2). This absolute and relative decline reflected, *inter alia*, the real increase in price of over 20 per cent between 1979 and 1980 and a decline in general economic activity (see Chapter 5).

The Museum responded to this challenge by a new focus on marketing. The Director's report for March 1981 stressed that Beamish was operating in a competitive environment and that any marketing effort should find 'what the visitor needs, satisfying the

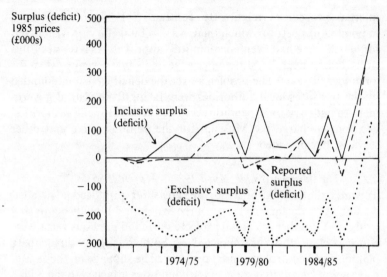

Surplus (deficit)
1985 prices
(£000s)

Source: Beamish records

Figure 2.3   Real surplus (deficit): three measures, 1970–1 to 1988–9

need with the right product at the right price in the right place, properly presented'.[42] The Museum also sought specialist advice from a tourism marketing consultant. Undoubtedly the first ever significant decline in visitor numbers stimulated this relatively intense interest in marketing. Up to 1980–2, it is probably fair to say that the orientation of the Museum was largely towards *production*. Certainly, the original aims were production orientated and did not refer to visitor needs or markets.

Subsequent years saw further strengthening of the marketing function. The 1983–4 budget allowed for a significant jump in marketing expenditure, which was again increased substantially in 1985–6.

Figure 2.3 shows the financial position of the Museum during this time. It provides three definitions of surplus (deficit) on the Museum's revenue account. The reported surplus (deficit) includes both loan charges and payments to the capital account as expenditure. The contribution from the constituent local authorities is included on the income side. The inclusive surplus (deficit) includes the local authorities' contribution, but disregards loan charges and payments to the capital account. The exclusive surplus (deficit) excludes the local authorities' contribution; it too disregards the loan charges and capital payments.

The figure shows that despite the fall in visitor numbers, the inclusive surplus (deficit) remained positive. This surplus was maintained for a number of reasons. First, as Table 2.1 shows, the local authorities substantially increased their revenue contribution in 1981–2. As a result the predicted deficit for that year did not materialize. Secondly, the Museum itself took measures to control costs. Vacant posts were frozen. Tighter financial controls and cost reduction measures were introduced (for example changes to the contracts of temporary workers virtually eliminated premium overtime rates). It is probably fair to say that without the intense economic pressures placed on the Museum it is unlikely that these changes would have come about so soon, or even at all.

Thirdly, two local authorities decided to cease charging the Museum for services rendered. Finally, despite some objections by local politicians, the real admission charge continued to increase: between the summer of 1981 and 1984, it rose by nearly 20 per cent.

Despite the financial challenges faced in the early 1980s there were also a number of encouraging signs. In May 1981 the MSC approved a new set of schemes. The newly established trust fund was also meeting some success: by June 1981 it reported that it had reached 80 per cent of its £500 000 target. Funds were forthcoming from other external sources. For example in March 1981 the European Regional Development Fund (ERDF) offered £200 000 for the development of the town area.[43] By 1983–4 61 per cent of the £324 700 planned capital expenditure was scheduled to come from outside bodies including the Trust.[44]

The Friends continued to maintain an active role in supporting the Museum, although the nature of that role was changing. In the early days they had provided vital support for the concept of the Museum and its initial development, and had been a crucial source of voluntary labour and capital. By the mid-1980s their activities were centring much more on the organization of special events at the Museum and on providing general 'moral' support.

In 1983 the Trust was given a new 'independent' look. When it was first formed it was dominated by local councillors, a characteristic which ensured continuing local political control, but which was not best suited to raising funds from industry and elsewhere.

Unfortunately, although the reconstituted Trust had trustees drawn from leading figures in industry and commerce, it effectively remained 'in limbo' because of resignations and illness between August 1983 and September 1986.

2.2.6   Recovery and growth: April 1985 – March 1990

At the beginning of the financial year 1985–6, the Museum recorded an increase in visitor numbers for the first time in several years: the April to June figures for 1985 were up 31 per cent over the previous year. As Figure 2.1 shows, visitor numbers in the calendar year 1985 were 40 per cent higher than in the previous year. As Figure 2.2 indicates, the recovery also expressed itself in a sharp rise in local market share.

Visitor numbers grew continuously in both absolute terms and relative to other local attractions throughout the second half of the decade. Important new developments including the official opening of the Town in 1985 and then, a year later, the visitor centre (see Chapter 5) played a role in stimulating visitor demand. General economic conditions also improved substantially. Furthermore the Museum of the Year Award in 1986 and the European Museum of the Year Award in 1987, almost certainly gave the standing of the Museum a boost. Partly because of its increased status, the Museum was drawing increasing numbers of visitors from outside the local area. In the summer of 1987 the proportion of British visitors coming from outside the North exceeded 50 per cent for the first time.

On the financial side, the Museum's position also became much stronger. As Table 2.1 shows, the local authority contribution to the revenue account remained fairly static in real terms but its *relative* importance as a source of income fell substantially. This development has given the Museum considerably more independence. Figure 2.3 shows that there was also great improvement on the revenue account, once the very substantial jump in 1986–7 in revenue expenditure on 'maintenance' – a category that may not significantly differ from capital expenditure – is taken into account. In 1988–9, an exclusive surplus was recorded for the first time in the Museum's history. This greatly improved financial position enabled the Museum to undertake a staff review, which led to an overall increase in full-time weekly and monthly staff of over 13 per cent between August 1988 and August 1989, with many weekly staff transferring to the monthly payroll.

On the capital side, funding received a welcome boost in September 1985 when Tyne and Wear County Council, then being abolished under local government reorganization, provided £680 000 towards the new visitor centre, which was also supported by £200 000 from the European Regional Development Fund. New developments in the late 1980s have included the rebuilding of a local school and chapel and the beginning of work on the tramway extension. Progress on the capital side was slower than originally anticipated because of the lower than expected level of funding available from the Trust.

Atkinson announced his retirement in early 1987. Fittingly, one of his last duties was the opening of a new visitor centre. The new Director, Peter Lewis, from Wigan Pier, took up his duties in June 1987.

2.3 Key factors in the Museum's development

2.3.1   The role of Atkinson and his staff
The growth of the Museum to its present scale and employment levels has clearly been complex. This section seeks to identify some of the key factors in this development.

There can be little doubt that without Atkinson's initial vision and his energy and enthusiasm for the Museum, and what it stood for in terms of Museum development generally,[45] the project would never have got off the ground in the way it did. He was not put off in the early days by the difficulties of securing financial support. Once the Museum was established he constantly pushed the local authorities to the limits of their financial commitment, a pressure which sometimes led him into conflict with councillors and officers. He mobilized widespread support for, and commitment to, his ideas. As a result the proposed Museum achieved a public profile which provided crucial backing for the initial negotiations with local authorities. He showed considerable skill in seeking out additional sources of funds and motivating staff. While adapting to changing circumstances and opportunities, he retained his underlying commitment to the fundamental concept of a Museum designed to provide a 'living' portrayal of the region's heritage. For example, he saw and exploited the increasing potential for fundraising that lay in the promotion of Beamish as a tourist attraction even though he himself would have regarded the latter term as an inaccurate reflection of the concept underlying the formation and development of the Museum.

Atkinson's passion did, however, bring its difficulties. His commitment to collect everything and anything that came his way inevitably created resource pressures on both labour and physical capacity. Atkinson's support for such an open-ended collecting policy was understandable: once a unique item is lost, it is lost for ever. Such a loss seemed all the more acute at a time of rapid social change such as the late 1960s. It is also the case that *ex ante* it is not always possible to identify those items which will prove to be particularly valuable reminders of an industrial or social heritage. Yet in a context where resources are under particularly heavy strain, some selectivity becomes all the more pressing.

As Section 2.2 showed, Atkinson also found himself in some conflict with the local authorities. This may have partly been due to his impatience with local authority procedures, some of which may have seemed an unnecessary bureaucratic impediment to the realization of an ideal. (As early as 1968 he had warned about possible adverse effects of local authority control on Museum operations.)[46] Although these tensions were at times considerable, Atkinson and these authorities shared an underlying commitment to the non-commercial nature and purpose of the Museum. Indeed it was this common perspective that was a key factor in the Museum's establishment and subsequent development.

Under Atkinson, a committed team was built up. In the early days particularly, working conditions and the scale of voluntary activities demanded a high level of loyalty to the underlying notion of a museum (a loyalty still evident today and in part reflected in the very low level of staff turnover). It is unlikely that the initial vision could have reached fruition without that commitment.

2.3.2   The local authorities

Atkinson would not have been given the chance to put his ideas into practice without financial assistance; and it is most unlikely that at the time the Museum was founded such assistance, and the employment resulting from it, would have been forthcoming in sufficient quantities from any source other than the local authorities. The role of the local authorities in launching the Museum was therefore critical. They also played an important financial role in ensuring its survival in the downturn of the early 1980s, as well as providing important technical expertise. But there were a number of important limitations associated with their role. First – and particularly in the early days – decision making was constrained by each local authority's desire to ensure that none of the other local authorities had a 'free ride'. Decision making also involved an iterative process that made progress difficult. The consortium type of arrangement underlying the Joint Committee was certainly an imaginative one but it inevitably had drawbacks. Although the committee was the formal vehicle for managing Beamish, it was the parent local authorities who ultimately made the resource decisions. Furthermore, the financial pressures faced by the local authorities and their vulnerability to central government economic policy made financial planning and management very difficult. For example, as the previous section has shown, local authorities were sometimes unable to make a firm commitment to capital financing until immediately before or after the start of the relevant year. This was particularly injurious to the planning of longer-term projects. Although the *relative* financial role of the local authorities on both capital and revenue account has reduced over the years, this should not detract from the important primary role that they played in the early days. It must be remembered too that their financial contribution is still substantial (see Table 2.1).

The local authorities also sought to keep prices low in the early years, a restriction which played an important part in the rapid growth of visitor numbers up to 1979, but which limited the financial resources available for expanding the labour force to respond adequately to such growth. Apart from some local authorities' political disposition against commercial types of operation they saw the Museum as 'belonging' to the region's people, who in turn were entitled to easy access. In this their views dovetailed with those of Atkinson.

2.3.3 Outside sources of assistance and funds

At the inception of the Museum, the Friends were an especially important form of financial, practical and moral assistance. Without the labour supplied by the Friends, the Museum would have been in great difficulty in running the early exhibitions. The first chairman provided important backing for the Museum's case for better funding and for a move away from relying on voluntary labour for routine tasks. The formation of the Friends was in part a reflection of the very widespread support that existed among the general public, support which Atkinson had played no small part in generating.

Outside funding for capital development has played an increasingly important role in the Museum's development, but it is unlikely that this has crowded out local authority funding.

2.3.4   External factors

It is important that the influence of Atkinson and his staff and of the local authorities should be placed firmly in context. At the time the Museum was first proposed and the working party undertook its task, social and industrial change seemed rapid. In such an environment any plan to preserve something of the past was likely to receive attention and backing, so the imaginative idea of an open-air museum was even more welcome. The greater emphasis on regional issues and policy in the mid-1960s also provided a sympathetic environment for the launching of what in effect was a regional museum. Furthermore, in the late 1960s central government interest in the development of museums was supportive. In the early 1970s it was tending to favour widening public appreciation rather than catering for the needs of specialized interests,[47] an emphasis which particularly favoured Beamish. On the other hand, central government restrictions did play some part in holding back the subsequent development of the Museum, particularly in the late 1970s. At a more general level Atkinson has also made the point that the strong community spirit in the North-East provided a solid base for a museum of the Beamish type.[48]

2.4   Conclusions

Despite the problems it has faced over the years, Beamish is now well established as a major museum and as one of the main tourist attractions in the North-East (see Table 1.3). On the evidence available, its growth in visitor numbers in recent years is better than that of many other major attractions in the region. While the Museum in its present form would probably not be commercially successful *overall*, the calculations in Johnson and Thomas (1989b) do suggest that on broader social criteria it currently generates a satisfactory return. So far it has successfully managed to combine the need to have tourism 'appeal' with the maintenance of historical authenticity.

As the previous sections have shown, Beamish as it exists today, and its current level of employment, are the product of an extensive range of complex and interacting factors. Some of these may rightly be regarded as more important than others. For example, the availability of the Beamish site, the commitment of Atkinson and (later) his staff, and the willingness of local authorities to provide financial support were all key elements in the formation of the Museum. The interdependence of these factors should also be recognized: no one element would have led to the development of the Museum without the contribution of the others.

The particular constellation of personal, institutional and environmental factors which led to the formation of Beamish and its subsequent development is unique and cannot of course be replicated. There can be little doubt that if the Museum were being launched today, the project would be tackled and developed in a different way at a different pace and with a different outcome. Employment growth would have followed a different pattern. The uniqueness of the Museum's development process means that any attempt to reach generally applicable conclusions must be regarded with some scepticism. Yet there are some elements in that process which suggest that some tentative generalizations may be obtained.

First, the Museum's history demonstrates the limitations of relying on local authority finance where anything other than a very short-term planning horizon is used. Any assessment of the limitations of local authority finance must be balanced by the high probability that in the case of Beamish – at least in its early years – no other source of finance would have been available.

Secondly, it is clear from experience at Beamish that a wide range of professional skills is necessary for the management function of a museum, whatever its objectives. This requirement becomes all the more pressing as the scale of operations increases. These skills do of course extend far beyond the curatorial function, although many curators may possess them. Well developed financial information systems and controls are also important.

Thirdly, museums operate in a market, whatever their objectives may be. Awareness of market trends and their determinants is crucial wherever visitor numbers and revenue have any relevance to museum management and the achievement of its objectives.

Experience at Beamish has shown that even where the product offered is innovatory, the appeal of such a product does not last for ever: a stream of new developments is required if visitor numbers are to be maintained and increased.

Finally, a museum like Beamish faces considerable difficulties in reconciling a multiplicity of objectives. Beamish has served a wide variety of purposes: the preservation and display of heritage; conservation and scholarship; education; the encouragement of a regional 'identity' and pride in the past; the provision of an enjoyable experience for local people and others from outside the region; and the generation of economic activity and employment. It is not difficult to see possible conflicts between these objectives. The resource trade-off between these objectives is a major task of management. How the trade-off is achieved will clearly have implications for employment in the Museum.

At the present time there are grounds for some optimism about the Museum's future and hence the employment it is likely to generate. Growth and development in the last few years, together with the public recognition received, has gone some way towards restoring the confidence lost in the downturn of the early 1980s. At the time of writing, prospects for expansion look good. However, as indicated earlier, Beamish is in a market competing with other claims on consumer expenditure. Furthermore, it cannot isolate itself from any product life cycle that may exist (see Chapter 6), and it is vulnerable to changes in general economic conditions. Both of these factors make constant adaptation and improvement of the visitor experience essential, if the Museum's development is to be sustained and the employment it offers increased.

Notes
The following abbreviations are used in these notes:

WPM – Working Party minutes
JCM – Joint Committee minutes

These documents are held by Durham County Council.

1. This chapter draws heavily on Johnson and Thomas (1989b), an abbreviated version of which was published as Johnson and Thomas (1990e).
2. Minutes of the Further Education Sub-Committee, 10 December 1958, p. 411. (The Bowes Museum Sub-Committee reported to this sub-committee.)
3. *The Times*, 18 June 1986.
4. See the report of the chief officers to the Museums Sub-Committee, 7 September 1965.

5. Minutes of the Further Education Sub-Committee, 18 March 1959, p. 530.
6. *Open Air Folk Museum; Report 1961.* This report is unsigned but originated from Atkinson.
7. The authors are grateful to Frank Atkinson for making this point. See McCrone (1969) for an account of regional policy during this period.
8. Minutes of the Museums Sub-Committee, 16 September 1966, p. 331.
9. Minutes of Working Party set up to consider the establishment of a Regional Open Air Museum: 4 October 1966.
10. WPM, 14 December 1966.
11. See the report of the Secretary on the Draft Agreement: 26 January 1967.
12. The two authorities were Middlesbrough County Borough Council and West Hartlepool County Borough Council (see WPM, 31 January 1967).
13. WPM, 14 December 1966.
14. WPM, 31 January 1967.
15. *Living History: An Open Air Museum for the North of England.*
16. *Northern Echo,* 27 June 1968.
17. See, for example, JCM, 6 February 1969.
18. County Councils of Durham and Northumberland, County Boroughs of Darlington, Gateshead, Hartlepool, Newcastle, South Shields and Teesside.
19. JCM, 18 September 1970.
20. JCM, 23 October 1970.
21. Report by the Treasurer and Museum Director, October 1970.
22. JCM, 11 December 1970.
23. The Museum does, however, continue to collect material which is of value for comparative purposes outside this target period.
24. Report by the Treasurer and the Museum Director, August 1971.
25. JCM, 10 September 1971.
26. JCM, 11 February 1972.
27. JCM, 10 December 1971.
28. Report of the Director, 8 September 1972.
29. JCM, 8 September 1972.
30. JCM, 8 December 1972.
31. JCM, 9 March 1973.
32. JCM, 28 September 1973.
33. JCM, 8 March 1974.
34. Minutes of the (Interim) Joint Committee, 10 July 1974.
35. JCM, 10 July 1974.
36. JCM, 4 April 1977.
37. *Internal Audit Report – Contract Procedures.* Report to the Joint Committee, 11 January 1980.
38. JCM, 11 April 1980.
39. *Financial Situation 1980/81,* 22 May 1980.
40. JCM, 18 September 1980.
41. *Revenue and Capital Programmes, 1980/81 – 1984/85,* 19 August 1980.
42. Report of the Museum Director to the Joint Committee, 6 March 1981.
43. JCM, 6 March 1981.
44. Joint Committee's Finance (and General Purposes) Subcommittee minutes, 3 March 1983.
45. See Atkinson (1968, 1975).
46. Ibid.
47. See Peacock and Godfrey (1974).
48. See Atkinson (1985).

3 The labour force at Beamish

3.1 Introduction

This chapter's brief discussion of certain aspects of the labour force at Beamish sets the scene for the assessment of the Museum's employment impact in Chapter 4. Section 3.2 looks at the importance of labour costs in the Museum's expenditure. Section 3.3 outlines some of the main characteristics of the structure of employment in the Museum, focusing on occupational breakdown, the division between weekly and monthly staff, and the employment catchment area. In Section 3.4 the growth of employment in the Museum over time, and the determinants of that growth, are examined.

3.2 Labour costs

The use of expenditure data from the Museum's accounts to estimate the relative importance of labour in the use of resources is not without limitations. The Beamish accounts do not incorporate resources made available without charge by other organizations. For example, much of the accountancy work for the Museum is undertaken without payment by Cleveland County Council. Secondly, some expenditure items in the accounts may not fully reflect the true opportunity cost of the resources involved. One illustration of this is the rental charged for the Beamish site: this is substantially lower than the value of the land in alternative uses. (Johnson and Thomas, 1989b). Yet these considerations are unlikely to affect the basic conclusion derived from the Museum's accounts, that labour is a key input. Figure 3.1, which is based on the accounts,[1] shows that employee costs, which include national insurance and pensions, have accounted for around 60 per cent of annual revenue expenditure over the past ten or so years. This proportion inevitably reflects the precise product 'mix' provided by the Museum, and the technology used to produce the different components of that mix. A key consideration in the balance of output provided is the distribution of resources between research and scholarly activities on the one hand, and the provision of visitor services on the other. Research and scholarship tend to be relatively highly labour intensive and to employ better-paid staff; it is hardly surpris-

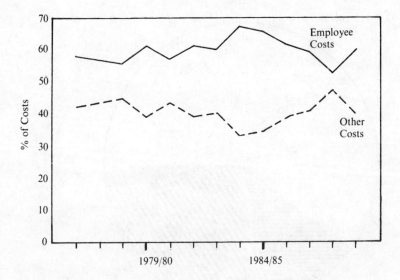

Source: Beamish accounts.

Figure 3.1 Beamish: breakdown of costs, 1976–7 to 1988–9

ing to find that the national museums, many of which have international research reputations, spend three-quarters of their budget on employee costs (MA, 1987: 174–5). Beamish is much less able, because of its sources of funding, to engage in research work. (Indeed, it appears to spend a *smaller* proportion of its budget on labour than the average local authority museum: MA, 1987: 175). The proportion of costs accounted for by personnel also reflects the particular mix of visitor services offered by Beamish. A greater emphasis on labour-intensive activities such as catering would raise this proportion.

A change in the technology of production may also alter the proportion. For example, interpretative services offered to visitors through audiovisual media would result in a lower proportion of total costs accounted for by labour than would be the case if the same services were provided through personal contact with Museum interpreters. Some change in production technology may mean that consumer activities are sometimes substituted for labour services.

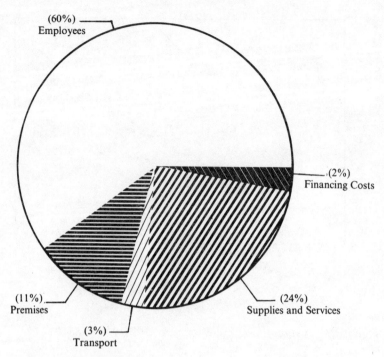

(60%)
Employees

(2%)
Financing Costs

(11%)
Premises

(3%)
Transport

(24%)
Supplies and Services

Source: Beamish accounts.

Figure 3.2   Beamish: breakdown of expenditure, 1988–9

(Visitors may have to read captions for themselves rather than have the exhibits explained to them.)[2]

Figure 3.2 shows the breakdown of revenue expenditure for 1988–9. Some substitution between the various elements shown may be possible – for example, the Museum may be able to compensate for a reduction in the number of interpreters by improving the quality of the buildings or by providing more exhibits, while keeping the overall quality of the visitor experience fairly constant, but the evidence from Figure 3.1. suggests that the Museum has not followed this route to any significant degree (see however Section 3.4 below).

It is interesting to note that although there has been some variation in the proportion of expenditure accounted for by labour costs (Figure 3.1) the other items of expenditure have individually shown more variability.[3] This may in part be due to the fact that it is usually more difficult to adjust labour rather than other costs to reflect variations in visitor numbers.

3.3 Some characteristics of the labour force

3.3.1 Sex and occupational breakdown

According to Table 3.1, about half the workers are female (49 per cent) and about half are male (51 per cent). The distribution of males and females across the different occupations simply reflects the occupational distribution of the sexes in the labour force in general. (Table 3.1 shows that 30 per cent of females are in white-collar occupations, i.e. supervisory, secretarial/clerical and professional, compared with only 15 per cent of males).

Almost 80 per cent of workers are manual and the rest are white-collar workers. This breakdown reflects the product mix and the technology of production that is employed.

Table 3.1 Occupational distribution of Beamish employees (percentages of total)

	Male	Female	Total
Manual workers	85	70	78
Unskilled	46	54	50
Semi-skilled	20	16	18
Skilled	18	0	9
Supervisory/clerical/technical	7	25	16
Supervisory	4	5	5
Secretarial/clerical	0	20	10
Technical	3	0	1
Professional	8	5	6
	100	100	100
	(51%)	(49%)	(100%)

Note: Figures may not add exactly because of rounding.

Source: Derived from a survey of employees at August 1988.

3.3.2 Weekly vs monthly staff

Figure 3.3 shows the breakdown of monthly paid and weekly paid staff for each year since the late 1970s. The monthly paid staff are

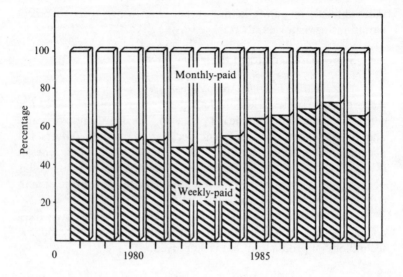

Source: Beamish records.

Figure 3.3   Proportion of weekly paid and monthly paid staff

mostly on permanent contracts and include all the professional staff,[4] and a core of secretarial, supervisory and skilled manual workers. The rest of the staff are weekly paid and for most of the 1980s virtually all of these were on short-duration contracts. They formed the most important part of the variable labour element in the workforce, and their numbers fluctuated seasonally (see below).

The distinction between weekly and monthly staff thus corresponds very loosely to that between variable and fixed labour costs. The downturn in visitor numbers at the beginning of the 1980s (see Figure 2.1) which emphasized the financial vulnerability of the Museum, led the Museum management to seek greater flexibility in its labour contracts and more control over the size of its labour force. It is only since 1989, after several years of growth in visitor numbers, that the management has been sufficiently confident to increase the proportion of monthly staff. However, this proportion has still not attained the level that prevailed in the late 1970s.

The seasonal fluctuations in demand which, as noted in Chapter 5, are largely dependent on the weather, lead to a pronounced seasonal pattern of employment: peak employment is 70 per cent higher than off-peak. (Visitor numbers fluctuate in a much more pronounced manner.)[5] The workers employed for the seasonal peak are mainly full-time: in 1989 only about 10 per cent of workers in August were part-time and, unlike some parts of the tourism and leisure industries,[6] there were virtually no casual workers (that is, workers employed for a few hours or days only).

Short-term contracts are typically for a 3 to 6-month period and workers are hired for specific non-interchangeable jobs. Such contracts are thought to provide a higher quality of labour than would be the case with casual hiring on a daily basis.

Although such contracts are better than casual hiring and, as noted earlier, provide management with more control over the labour force, they have few if any benefits for employees, many of whom have been continuously employed for a number of years on back-to-back short-term contracts. Clearly, such employees face considerable uncertainty of employment and income.[7]

3.3.3 The Museum's employment catchment area

Travel-to-work distances are typically short: 48 per cent of workers live within a 3-mile radius of the Museum and 94 per cent within 10 miles, as shown in Figure 3.4. This pattern of residence, which is similar for all grades of staff, suggests that the direct impact of employment is fairly concentrated on the immediate labour market area.

3.4 The growth of employment

3.4.1 The overall picture

The number of employees grew substantially from 42 in 1978 to 148 in 1989,[8] but this growth has been uneven and has been markedly different for different types of staff (see Figure 3.5). This figure shows that weekly paid staff have grown dramatically in numbers since the early 1980s, while numbers of monthly paid staff have until recently remained fairly constant. Some of the reasons for this development have already been outlined.

3.4.2 Employment, visitor numbers and admission revenues

Although defining the 'output' produced by Beamish is not a straightforward task, visitor numbers and admissions revenue are

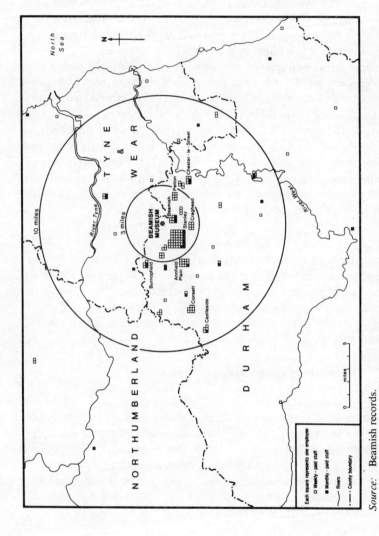

Source: Beamish records.

Figure 3.4 Employees of Beamish Museum, August 1988 – distribution by place of residence

44

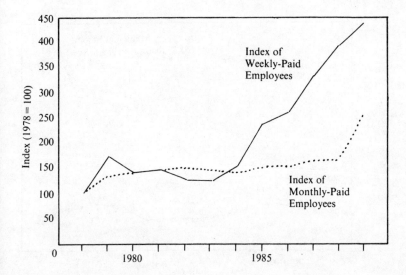

Source: Beamish records.

Figure 3.5   The growth in the number of staff

taken for the purposes of this discussion as indicators of the scale of output.

Figure 3.6 shows that the number of staff has grown more rapidly than the number of visitors but less rapidly than admission income (in constant prices). There has thus been an increase in the labour intensity of output: Figure 3.7 shows the downward drift in the number of visitors per employee from well over 5 000 at the end of the 1970s to about 3 500 by the mid-1980s. This increased labour intensity cannot, however, be interpreted as a fall in labour productivity,[9] because revenue per worker has been maintained or increased (as shown in Figure 3.7) and this suggests that the average revenue product has not declined.[10] Nor is the increased labour intensity likely to be the result of a changing mix of labour and other inputs (for example, in response to changes in the relative price of inputs or changes in technology).

The most likely explanation of the growth in labour intensity is to be found in the nature of Beamish and its exhibits. The exhibits, which are the framework for providing the 'Beamish experience', are

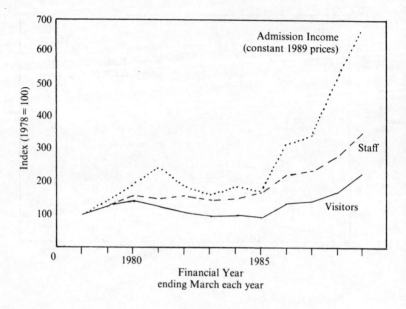

Source: Beamish records.

Figure 3.6   *The growth of staff, visitors and admission income (index numbers 1978 = 100)*

in place with their attendant staff (for example interpreters, demonstrators, maintenance and security staff). When visitor numbers increase, the number of exhibits increases (or existing exhibits are enhanced) with a consequent increase in staff.[11] However, when the number of visitors falls there is a ratchet: the number of exhibits and staff in place does not fall. Thus, in periods of visitor downswing the labour intensity per visitor rises, and this is not reversed in the upswing.

This situation is clearly illustrated in Figure 3.8. During the early 1980s when visitor numbers fell there was no corresponding fall in employment, and during the later 1980s when the number of visitors rose, employment resumed its growth.

In terms of the composition of staff, it is not surprising to find that most of the covariation of employment with visitor numbers and with admission revenue is among weekly paid rather than monthly

The vertical scale shows Admission Revenue ('000) per employee
in constant 1989 prices, and Visitors ('000) per employee.

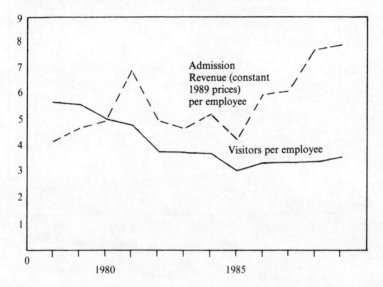

Financial Year ending March each year

Source: Beamish records.

*Figure 3.7   Visitors per employee and admission revenue per
employee*

paid staff. This corresponds to the categorization made in Section
3.3.2 that the former correspond broadly to variable labour costs
and the latter to fixed labour cost. Appendix 2 suggests that in
approximate terms an extra 4 000 visitors is associated with the
employment of one additional weekly paid employee, whereas the
figure for monthly paid staff is about 22 000 visitors.[12] Similarly, if
the additional revenue associated with additional members of staff is
examined then the figure is approximately £11 900 for weekly paid
staff and about £62 500 for monthly paid staff. The data are not
adequate to permit a proper examination of the growth of employment over time but the results presented here do suggest some
interesting relationships.[13]

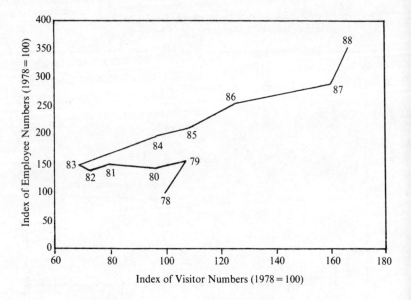

Source: Beamish records.

Figure 3.8   Relationship between visitor numbers and the number of employees, 1978–88

3.5   Conclusion

This chapter has demonstrated the importance of the labour force in the activities of the Museum and has outlined some key characteristics of that labour force and its growth over recent years. The relationship between employment in the Museum and visitor numbers and admission revenues was also briefly explored. What the chapter has not done is to examine the *difference* the presence of Beamish makes to employment in the reference area. This issue is the focus of the next chapter.

Notes
1. These accounts include only the costs associated with the employment of the Museum's own labour force. In most of the years covered in Figure 3.1, there were, in addition to the Museum's own employees, a substantial number of workers (65 in 1987 taking the average for the whole year) employed at the Museum under the Manpower Services Commission's scheme. Under this scheme grants were paid to enable workers to be hired temporarily for projects which would not otherwise be undertaken. The scheme ceased in 1988 and the

Museum has since made only very limited use of the subsequent policy initiative, Employment Training. Workers on the MSC scheme have not been included in the totals of employment because they were entirely dependent on special government subsidy (which was not museum specific) and they were not substitutes for the Museum's ordinary employees.

2. For some discussion on the substitution of consumers for labour, which may have effects analogous to the substitution of capital for labour, see Medlik (1988).

3. The coefficient of variation for labour costs as a percentage of total costs for the financial years ending 1977 to 1989, was only 6.3 per cent compared with the following figures for other costs: premises, 18.8 per cent; transport, 33.4 per cent; supplies and services, 54.5 per cent; establishment expenses, 50.9 per cent; financing costs, 68.1 per cent.

4. There were a very few monthly paid temporary workers on short-duration contracts. These were staff engaged for particular projects, for example an education officer, a technical officer engaged in restoration work, and an architect, but their employment depended on special earmarked funds provided by the MSC and was not directly related to the volume of business.

5. In 1989, for example, visitor numbers in August were 13 times greater than in February (and 29 times greater than in January) compared with August employment, which was 1.7 times greater than February employment. This indicates the relatively fixed character of labour over the course of the year.

6. See Metcalf (1987) for a detailed account of the incidence of seasonal and casual work in the tourism and leisure industries.

7. It is perhaps not surprising therefore to find that almost 60 per cent of weekly paid staff are members of households with other earners (the proportion is a little higher for women).

8. See note 1.

9. For an examination of aggregate trends in tourism productivity and the employment implications see Medlik (1988).

10. The average revenue product of labour can of course change quite independently of changes in the average physical product so it must be acknowledged that rising revenue per worker could be consistent with falling labour productivity.

11. The number of staff actually increases less than proportionately. Some care is needed with the arguments developed in the text because a simple examination of time series data does not take account of the fact that there may be changes in managerial policy over time to make exhibits more labour intensive.

12. These and the following figures in the text are based on the reciprocal of the coefficient and on the independent variable (visitor numbers) shown in the regression reported in Appendix 2.

13. It is tempting to view the figures of additional visitors per employee, quoted in the text, as the marginal product of labour, and the figures quoted of the additional revenue per employee as the gross marginal revenue product. This would, however, be inappropriate because the time series regression used for these estimates takes no account of other changes, for example in other inputs or technology, which may have taken place.

4 The Museum's employment impact

4.1 The key question

Estimation of the employment impact of the Museum requires an answer to the following question:

> What *difference* does the presence of the Museum make to the level and type of employment in the reference area?

(The definition of the reference area was discussed in Section 1.4.)

The above question requires a consideration of what the level of employment would have been if the Museum had not existed. The framework for answering this question is provided in Sections 4.2 and 4.3. The results of the empirical study are given in Section 4.4.

Most attention here is focused on the *number* of jobs which is generated by the Museum. There are, however, two wider considerations which deserve mention although they are not dealt with explicitly in this study. The first requires recognition of the fact that simply counting the number of jobs ignores the wide variation that exists in the economic characteristics of jobs. Different structures of jobs may have very different effects on local economic activity, on the level of measured unemployment and on local welfare. Whether jobs with different characteristics, for example unskilled casual jobs and skilled permanent jobs, should be counted equally will depend partly on the exact purpose of the evaluation.

From a social welfare perspective it is important to take account of the fact that jobs may differ greatly in their 'quality'. It is now well recognized that there are growing numbers of so-called precarious jobs in society which have, for instance, low skill requirements, low pay and benefits, very limited statutory employment protection, no union recognition agreements, little or no discretion given to workers in decisions on how the job should be done, and short-term contracts. These differ markedly from jobs offering stable permanent employment with good pay and conditions determined through collective bargaining arrangements.[1] It does not necessarily follow that the 'poor' jobs are not capable of contributing to social welfare – there may be a preference on the part of some workers for part-time jobs which are nearby and which require little in the way of training or other qualifications, over higher-paying jobs which have stringent entry requirements and which are full time. It would normally be the case, however, that such 'poorer' jobs should be given less weight than the 'better' jobs.

A related issue concerns the units in which employment is estimated. It is sometimes more useful to count employment in terms of person-years rather than the number of workers of all kinds who are on the books at a particular time. Some museums, for example, have a large pool of casual peak-period workers from which they draw as necessary, but the pool of available workers would often give an exaggerated picture of the actual flow of employee services hired.

In this study no account has been taken of the quality of jobs though wherever possible jobs have been counted in terms of full-time equivalents.

The second wider issue which warrants consideration is that there may be some very general positive effects on employment in the reference area which it is not possible to quantify. Chapter 1 has already suggested that the Museum makes a contribution to the general attractiveness of the area by promoting and enhancing the regional profile. This in turn may lead to more inward investment which would have an effect on employment. Although it would be virtually impossible to estimate the size of any such effects which were specifically attributable to Beamish this does not mean that they do not exist. They have, however, been ignored in the present study.

4.2 Employment concepts and measures

4.2.1 Direct, indirect and induced activities
The terminology used in this study identifies direct, indirect and induced activities. *Direct activities* are of two kinds: the key activity (Beamish Museum) and associated activities. The key activity is the project whose employment is being studied. All activity *inside* the boundaries of the project is included. The associated activities are the result of final expenditure *outside* the boundaries of the key activity which can be attributed to the key activity. Visitors to the key activity often spend, for example, on meals, accommodation, shopping and other tourist attractions, and local and central government may invest in infrastructure and other facilities related to the key activity.

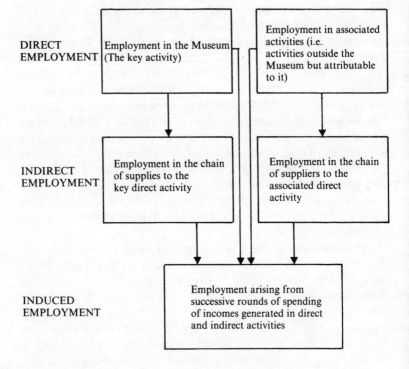

Figure 4.1   The economic benefits of the Museum

Indirect activity is that occurring in the chain of suppliers of goods and services to direct activities. It should be noted that this distinction between direct and indirect activity occurs only because the direct activities are not completely vertically integrated.[2] If there were backward integration right down the chain of suppliers then all activities would be direct and no indirect activities would exist. There will be indirect activity stemming from the direct activity in both the key activity and the associated activity.

Induced activity is that which results from successive rounds of expenditure out of incomes generated from direct and indirect activity. These rounds of spending are referred to as the multiplier effects.

The economic benefits of the Museum are in the form of employment in each kind of activity just described. Figure 4.1 summarizes the position.[3]

4.2.2 Gross and net employment

It is useful to distinguish between the gross and net employment (designated subsequently as E and N respectively) generated by the key activity in the reference area. Estimates of gross employment assume that no demand (and hence no employment) is diverted from elsewhere in the reference area. Net employment is gross employment *less* that employment which has been 'transferred' from elsewhere in the reference area as a result of demand diversion. The latter is considered in more detail below.

Gross employment: the framework Gross employment may be divided into direct, indirect and induced employment corresponding to the three types of activity described above. Direct employment is that occurring in the direct activities. It may be written

$$E_I = S_K e_K + \sum_i S_{A_i} e_{A_i} \qquad (4.1)$$

where E_I is direct employment, S is the sales revenue, e is the employment-sales ratio, and the subscripts K and A refer to the key and associated activities respectively. In practice it may sometimes be easier to observe employment directly rather than estimate it via sales. Equation (4.1) has nevertheless been written in this form because it shows, firstly, the conceptual relevance of sales and provides a consistent treatment with subsequent equations, and secondly, estimates of associated employment are sometimes more easily obtained indirectly through sales.[4] To obtain S_{A_i} in equation (4.1) it is necessary to assess how far sales in activity i can be attributed to the key activity. If S_i is the total sales of activity i, then S_{A_i} may be defined as

$$S_{A_i} = S_i \alpha_i \qquad 0 < \alpha_i \leqslant 1$$

where α_i is the *attribution factor*, i.e. the proportion of sales in activity i which would not have occurred without the presence of the key activity. Note that S_i refers to the sales in *all* activities in the reference area (except the key activity, which is designated separately). In the vast majority of cases these will be entirely independent of Beamish, i.e. $\alpha_i = 0$. The definition of associated activity is where $\alpha_i > 0$.

Sales in activity i may be generated by two types of demand. Type

(1) is that which would not have arisen if the key activity had not existed; type (2) demand is the remainder, and comprises all the demand for activity i which would have occurred even if the key activity had not existed. Sales generated by type (1) demand are wholly attributable to the key activity.[5] Those generated by type (2) are not normally attributable to the key activity (see below). Many activities will typically have a mixture of types (1) and (2) demand, hence α_i will lie between 0 and 1. It should be noted that type (1) demand may be generated by visitors to the reference area who may not actually visit the key activity, even though they are induced to visit the reference area because of the latter. This apparent anomaly arises because the decision to visit the reference area, and the decision over what activities actually to visit, are separate and subject to different influences.[6]

It was indicated above that sales from type (2) demand are not *normally* attributable to the key activity. However there may be some instances where without the sales arising from type (1) demand, the activity would not be viable and would cease to exist. In these instances, the sales arising from even type (2) demand would be attributable to the key activity.

Indirect employment is that which arises in the indirect activity. The first round of indirect employment, in the reference area, is that in the immediate suppliers to the direct activity. Thus

$$\text{First-round indirect employment} = S[p(1-m_f)]e$$

where p is the proportion of sales revenue which is spent on supplies, and m_f is the marginal propensity of firms to import supplies into the reference area. These suppliers will in turn spend on supplies to give second-round indirect employment, and so on as shown below.[7]

$$
\begin{aligned}
\text{Indirect employment} \quad \text{Round } 1 &= S[p(1-m_f)]e \\
2 &= S[p(1-m_f)]^2e \\
3 &= S[p(1-m_f)]^3e \\
&\ \ \vdots \\
n &= S[p(1-m_f)]^ne \\
\text{Total } (n=\infty) &= S[\{1-p(1-m_f)\}^{-1}-1]e
\end{aligned}
$$

Total indirect employment, E_{II}, can be written with subscripts (previously defined) as

$$E_{II} = S_K\{[1 - p_K(1 - m_{f,K})]^{-1} - 1\}e_K +$$
$$\sum_i S_{A_i}\{[1 - p_{A_i}(1 - m_{f,A_i})]^{-1} - 1\}e_{A_i} \qquad (4.2)$$

For convenience the subscripts may be dropped from equations (4.1) and (4.2) and they can be written as

$$E_I = Se$$
$$E_{II} = S[\{1 - p(1 - m_f)\}^{-1} - 1]e$$

thus the total of direct plus indirect employment is

$$E_{I+II} = S[1 - p(1 - m_f)]^{-1}e \qquad (4.3)$$

Induced employment, which occurs in induced activity, may be calculated as follows. The total revenue from sales in direct and indirect activity is given by dividing equation (4.3) by e. The fraction of this which is paid out as personal incomes, i.e. payments to factor owners, forms an appropriate multiplicand, given that our concern is with employment generation. This multiplicand is then used to calculate total spending in the reference area by applying the local spending multiplier. This total spending can then be multiplied by e to get the total employment. This total employment will, however, include E_{I+II} because these were the jobs that were associated with the initial incomes which begat the multiplier process; they must be deducted if the concern is only with induced employment. Induced employment, E_{III}, is thus

$$E_{III} = BS[1 - p(1 - m_f)]^{-1}ke - S[1 - p(1 - m_f)^{-1}]e \qquad (4.4)$$

where B is the proportion of the firms' revenues which are paid out as personal incomes (i.e. factor payments) and k is the local income multiplier. There are many computations of the local multiplier (Archer, 1977): the version adopted here is expressed as follows

$$k = [1 - c(1 - t)(1 - m_c)]^{-1} \qquad (4.5)$$

where c is the marginal propensity to consume, t is the marginal direct tax rate and m_c is the marginal propensity of consumers to import from outside the reference area.[8]

The total gross employment effect of the direct activity may be found by inserting (4.5) into (4.4) and adding (4.3) to give

$$E = E_{I+II+III} = BS[1 - p(1 - m_f)]^{-1}[1 - c(1 - t)(1 - m_c)]^{-1}e \quad (4.6)$$

Gross employment: further considerations The framework presented here for estimating gross employment embodies a number of simplifying assumptions. Firstly, the calculations assume constant coefficients. In the calculation of the indirect employment, for example, the values of p, m_f and e in each of the backward linkages in the chain of suppliers are taken as constant. A similar point applies to the multiplier used in the estimation of induced employment. Sinclair and Sutcliffe (1978: 181) have noted that this assumption is 'usually made since it would not be feasible to estimate the values appropriate to each individual round and it permits the simple summing of a geometric series, which is basic to the multiplier formula', though elsewhere the same individuals (1982: 324) have argued that 'the values of the first round propensities to withdraw are likely to be particularly atypical' and there is thus a need for separate estimation of the coefficients in the first, second and subsequent rounds.

Secondly, the formulae presented above incorporate marginal relationships though in practice average coefficients have to be used. This practice assumes that there is always surplus capacity to meet future demand. The multiplier calculations here assume no constraints.[9] (Similarly, in the labour market it is assumed that there are no constraints in filling vacancies so the terms 'jobs' and 'employment' may be used interchangeably.)

Thirdly, a similar argument concerns disaggregation. Sinclair and Sutcliffe (1982) note that the propensities to withdraw may be different for the recipients of income from profits and from wages. Where it is possible to take account of this it is desirable to do so. Disaggregation by type of firm is also relevant.[10] Different firms may, for example, have different propensities to spend on local suppliers and may have different employment–sales ratios. At least in the first round this should be acknowledged; thereafter it may make less difference to the final results. The first round is especially significant in the calculations, and since the 'income generation is of greater magnitude than that of any other round it is particularly important that first round effects should be estimated correctly' (Sinclair and Sutcliffe, 1978: 177).

Fourthly, no account is taken of inter-regional feedbacks. In practice, however, for the study of a single project, the flow of spending on suppliers *outside* the reference area which then spend back in the reference area on *their* suppliers, is likely to be small.

Finally, in the presentation above, little explicit attention was given to the time pattern of employment generation. The calculation of the total employment effect is an end-point estimation where it is assumed, for instance, that the whole chain of indirect spending is in place and can be used for calculating the consequent induced spending which, again, is assumed to have been completed.[11]

Net employment The calculation of net employment requires an estimate of the extent of demand diversion. If expenditure on the direct activities is diverted from other activities in the reference area then any employment in the key activity may simply be transferred from these other activities in the reference area with no net gain in employment in the area.[12] A few minor qualifications need to be made to this proposition. First, when expenditure is switched from one activity to another the net employment change will only be zero if the employment loss in the former equals the employment gain in the latter. However, the 'loser' and 'gainer' activities may differ in their employment–sales ratios so that a given expenditure diversion may cause more (less) employment to be lost in the activity from which the expenditure comes than is gained in the activity to which the expenditure is switched. In the absence of detailed data, constancy of employment–sales ratios is assumed in this study.

Secondly, the transfer of employment may not be directly from the firm(s) from which expenditure has been diverted. There may be a long chain of bumping in the labour market with many intermediate transfers but the end of the process will be no net gain in employment nor any change in the level of unemployment.[13] Thirdly, it may be argued that all expenditure has alternative uses and in this sense all expenditure is diverted. The crucial concern in the present analysis is the expenditure which is diverted *within the reference area*: expenditure which is switched from outside the area is not treated as diverted in this study. Such an approach is of value where the localized impact of a policy is being evaluated. This issue of whether all expenditure is ultimately diverted is discussed further below.

Net employment is gross employment after allowing for the proportion of expenditure which is diverted, δ, i.e. $N = (1 - \delta)E$. Thus, if all expenditure is diverted then net employment which is attributable to the key activity is zero. Employment in that activity is simply displacing employment elsewhere. The relationship between net and gross employment may not however depend only on expenditure switching in the product market. The state of the labour market may also be relevant. If, for example, the labour market were very tight and there were no unemployment then no net increase in employment would be possible. Labour market conditions may be incorporated into the above analysis by writing

$$N = (1 - \delta)\lambda E \qquad 0 \leqslant \delta \leqslant 1$$
$$0 \leqslant \lambda \leqslant 1 \qquad (4.7)$$

where λ is the measure of labour market slack specified as follows:

$$\lambda = 1 \text{ for } U \geqslant E$$
$$0 < \lambda < 1 \text{ for } U < E$$
$$\lambda = 0 \text{ for } U = 0$$

where U is the stock of suitably qualified unemployed persons in the reference area.[14] It is apparent that $N \to 0$ as $\delta \to 1$ and/or $\lambda \to 0$. In most analyses the concern will be with the size of N, but it is worth noting that even if N is small there may still be some welfare gain if the new *structure* of employment in the reference area increases individual welfare. For example, the substitution of say, part-time for full-time jobs may match local labour market 'needs' more exactly.

Equations (4.6) and (4.7) may be combined to show net employment from the key activity, i.e.

$$N = (1-\delta)\lambda BS[1 - p(1 - m_f)]^{-1}[1 - c(1 - t)(1 - m_c)]^{-1}e \quad (4.8)$$

4.3   The framework summarized
The argument can be best summarized from equation (4.7). If it is assumed that there is no labour market constraint on recruitment, which seems realistic, i.e. $\lambda = 1$, and it is noted that

$$E = K + A$$

where K is direct employment in the key activity and A is all additional employment (i.e. direct employment in associated activity plus all indirect and all induced activity) then it follows that

$$N = (1 - \delta)(K + A) \qquad (4.9)$$

Thus it is evident that net employment is negatively related to the size of the diversion factor and positively related to the size of employment in the key activity and to the total of all additional employment. From a policy point of view δ, K and A are variables which in principle it might be possible to alter to raise net employment. These matters are explored a little further in Chapter 6.

4.4 The results

The general framework outlined in the previous section has been used to establish the gross and net impact of Beamish. The details of all the calculations are presented in Appendix 3. The estimates of gross employment are shown in Table 4.1.[15] The direct jobs in Beamish represent about 60 per cent of the total jobs generated in the North-East as a result of the Museum's presence, i.e. there is an employment multiplier of 1.64: for every job directly in the Museum a further 0.64 of a job ensues in the region.[16]

The calculation of net employment requires adjustment of the gross employment figure to allow for the fact that for these employment gains there might be corresponding losses in employment elsewhere in the reference area if expenditure in Beamish and associated activities is diverted from other activities. The precise methods of calculating the diverted employment are presented in Appendix 3. The calculations suggest that the diversion factor might be very powerful: about three-quarters of the jobs are diverted, i.e. 195 jobs out of gross employment of 256 are displaced from within the region, leaving net employment as 61 jobs.

Table 4.1   *Gross employment impact in the North-East of Beamish Museum: number of jobs*

	Key activity (Beamish)	Associated activity	Total
Direct	156 (61)	31 (12)	187 (72)
Indirect	41 (16)	4 (2)	45 (18)
Induced	20 (8)	4 (2)	24 (10)
	217 (84)	39 (16)	256 (100)

Note: Figures in brackets show percentage of total gross employment. Totals may not add exactly because of rounding.

Table 4.2   Summary of employment impact in the North-East of Beamish Museum, 1989

	Number of jobs	% of jobs in Museum
Direct employment in Museum	156	100
plus additional jobs[1]	100	64
GROSS EMPLOYMENT	256	164
minus diverted jobs	195	125
NET EMPLOYMENT	61	39

1. Direct jobs in the associated activities, plus all indirect plus all induced jobs.

The results of the whole exercise are shown in Table 4.2. It is clear that the estimated diverted employment is very large indeed: it is greater than the additional jobs created, so that net employment is less than the number of jobs in Beamish itself.

4.5 Conclusion

This chapter has provided a conceptual framework and some estimates of the gross and net effects of Beamish Museum on the local economy. In this conclusion some comments are made on the quality and interpretation of the results.

The results inevitably embody a certain amount of judgement, and several assumptions about appropriate values of some of the parameters (for example in the multiplier calculations) have been made. It must also be recognized that crucial concepts such as attribution and diversion are hard to estimate.[17] The general conclusion does, however, seem fairly robust: additional jobs are created but these are likely to be fully, or more than, offset by the displacement of jobs elsewhere in the region.[18] There are of course some limitations to the results. It was noted earlier in the chapter that in some ways they may underestimate the true employment-generating capacity of the Museum because wider possibilities such as enhancing the flow of inward investment in the region have not been taken into account. Moreover, no account was taken of the qualitative aspects of the employment generated.

One of the major concerns in interpreting the results is the question of whether gross or net employment is of most interest. From the standpoint of society as a whole it is almost certainly net employment, that is, after taking account of displacement effects elsewhere. On this basis Beamish results suggest that the net employment-generating effect is modest. Table 4.2 showed that the *net* employment was only about 40 per cent of the employment in Beamish. However, it would be wrong to draw the conclusion that this is a 'poor' performance. Taking net employment, as defined in this study, is a particularly stringent way of assessing the impact. If similar tests were applied to a wide range of different projects it would not be surprising if they also had seemingly limited impact.[19] In practice, in most policy discussions, comparisons across different projects are often in terms of gross employment.

One factor of crucial importance in interpreting estimates of net employment is the size of the reference area. The amount of diverted employment is likely to increase as the reference area expands. This point is of some importance from the point of view of public bodies providing funds. For example, local authorities and the Treasury might have very different views on the net impact because they are concerned with different reference areas. An illustrative calculation of the relevance of the size of the reference area for estimating the net impact is presented in Appendix 4.

Notes
1. The 'quality' dimension of jobs has been receiving increasing recognition, and there is a growing body of literature which examines the growth of precarious jobs as a permanent feature of the workforce. See for example Rodgers and Rodgers (1989) for a good discussion.
2. In practice it seems unlikely that there would ever be complete vertical integration. The supply of basic services such as water and electricity, for example, are rarely provided by firms meeting final consumers' needs.
3. The induced employment shown in Figure 4.1 could have been separated into that which is dependent on the incomes and employment generated from the key direct plus key indirect and that which is dependent on the associated direct plus associated indirect. It has been shown in the figure as a single box because the employment estimates presented later in this chapter are based on a calculation of induced employment which treats all the key and associated direct and indirect activity as a single entity.
4. The emphasis on sales revenue in equation (4.1) should not of course obscure the fact that in addition to expenditure by consumers, capital expenditure also generates jobs. For expositional convenience this has been subsumed under S in the presentation throughout the text.
5. It is important to note that the attribution factor is estimated on a *ceteris paribus* basis, with the key activity being viewed as the marginal activity. Thus while it may be true that a visitor generating sales at a number of activities in the reference area would not have visited the latter if *any one* of these activities had not existed, this fact of itself is irrelevant to an assessment of the impact that the

key activity makes. Studies could of course be made of the impact of the other activities, in which case similar reasoning would apply. Clearly, it would not be appropriate to examine such activity in turn and *then* to aggregate the results. The attribution factor for the key activity itself is, of course, 1.

6. Thus an individual may for example decide to visit the reference area because he/she knows that such a visit would permit several attractions – one of which is the key activity – to be visited, but may in the event not visit the key activity.

7. It should be noted that the -1 appears in this expression for the sum of indirect employment because the first term of this geometric progression is $S[p(1-m_t)]e$, rather than Se, since direct employment $(E_1 = Se)$ is not included.

8. This formulation assumes that consumption is a function of disposable income, $Y(1-t)$, and that imports are a function of consumption rather than income. The conceptual issues in the definition of local tourism multipliers, and in particular the correct definition of initial leakages, have received attention in the literature. See for example Sinclair and Sutcliffe (1978, 1982) and Archer (1982).

9. See Wanhill (1988) for a model which incorporates capacity constraints.

10. Some writers have presented formulae which have attempted to spell out the full disaggregation across firms. In some cases, however, the clarity of their exposition is questionable: see for example, the appendices to the supplementary reports to the Myerscough (1988) study.

11. There may of course be a strong policy interest in the short-run effects. See Sinclair and Sutcliffe (1987) for a model for calculating truncated multipliers for a *time* period.

12. For a discussion of a slightly different concept of employment displacement, arising when incoming firms to an area compete labour away from other firms, see Harris *et al.* (1987).

13. This assumes that the labour force is of constant size, i.e. there is no change in the reference area population nor in participation rates.

14. They must be of the desired skill level and in the right location (i.e. the wage minus travel costs must exceed the unemployment benefit level by an amount equal to the reservation wage).

15. These figures which are identical to those in Johnson and Thomas (1991a) differ from earlier estimates (Johnson and Thomas, 1989a, 1990d) not only because they refer to a later year but also because more accurate evidence, based on a visitor survey, was used to calculate associated employment.

16. The use of this ratio has been criticized, see Archer (1984), but it has value in our present context.

17. The visitor survey used in this research (see Appendix 5) is likely to provide the most accurate information available on the attribution and diversion issues. Indeed, whatever the limitations of such surveys, there is no superior feasible way of estimating visitors' actual and hypothetical expenditure. Confidence in the Beamish visitor survey results is enhanced by the fact that the patterns of expenditure revealed and the differences across different categories of visitor, for example day trippers and those who were staying in the region, are in line with expectations.

18. The sensitivity of the results to alternative parameter values has been examined in Johnson and Thomas (1989c).

19. It is quite possible for net employment to be negative if more jobs are lost than gained. Local hypermarkets, for example, may often have a negative employment effect if they displace local retail sales by operations with a higher sales–employment ratio (i.e. less labour intensive). This may be offset to some extent by the generation of extra retail sales because of lower prices, which increase real incomes.

5 Visitor demand*

5.1 Introduction

It is evident from the previous chapters that the number of visitors has a key influence on the Museum's employment impact. Not surprisingly, as Chapter 4 has shown, employment in the Museum itself is positively related to the number of visitors, although the relationship is clearly a complex one. The employment in associated activities is all dependent on visitors. The employment in indirect and induced activities is of course determined by the level of activity and behaviour of the key and associated direct activities and so indirect and induced employment is also related to visitor flows. The size of visitor flows is also relevant for local authority support and hence the employment which that support generates. To the extent that such support is seen as a kind of 'launching aid' (the support was much greater in the early years), a measure of its success is the growth in the number of visitors.

Because of the importance of visitor numbers as a determinant of the scale of the employment impact, this chapter looks more closely at visitor characteristics and at the pattern of visiting. It also presents an econometric study of visitor numbers over time. It should however be remembered that visitor expenditure (number of visitors *multiplied by* the average spend) may sometimes be a more relevant variable than the number of visitors alone. The modelling in this chapter deals only with visitor numbers, although the results in the previous chapter depend critically on estimates of expenditure.

It should be noted at the outset that the number of visitors and the 'product' that they receive are interdependent. Visitors are themselves part of the 'Beamish experience' and their numbers affect the average quality of that experience. Most obviously, as the number of visitors grows to the point where the Museum becomes crowded, the average quality of the experience declines.[1] There is more queuing, visitor facilities become stretched and there is pressure on visitors to complete their viewing of an exhibit in a shorter period. Even if the concern is with a situation which falls well short of visitors to

*Part of this chapter draws on joint work with Adrian Darnell, whose help is gratefully acknowledged: see Darnell *et al.* (1989, 1990).

63

Beamish having a detrimental effect on average product quality, it seems clear that interdependence of the number of visitors and what they are getting does exist. (It may also be that the quality of experience decreases if there are 'too few' visitors.) In this chapter there is little attempt formally to unravel this interdependence and the focus is simply on the flow of visitors *per se*.

In Section 5.2 the characteristics of visitors and the pattern of visiting is described. (Much of the discussion draws on a visitor survey, some details of which are given in Appendix 5.) This is followed in Section 5.3 by some brief remarks on trends in visitor numbers and the seasonal nature of demand. In Section 5.4 a model of visitor flows is presented. Attention is focused on a single equation demand model based on elementary economic theory.[2] Such a model, despite its limitations, can provide some understanding of visitor flows. (It may also be of value as a management tool and for forecasting.)[3]

5.2   Visitor characteristics and the pattern of visiting

It is important to place the formal modelling of visitor flows within the context of fuller information on visitor characteristics and activities. It is useful, for instance, to identify different types of visitor (for example distinguishing day trippers from other visitors, and looking at the socioeconomic composition of the flow of visitors) because their behaviour, particularly in terms of spending in the region, differs considerably. Furthermore, there are several issues such as the rate of decay of the visitor experience (which will influence the frequency of repeat visiting) and the potential for increasing both visitor numbers and the average spend by visitors, which require knowledge of the pattern of visiting. For instance, the duration of a visit to the Museum, the number of exhibits visited, and the home region of visitors, are all relevant in building up an understanding of the visitor experience and hence of visitor flows.

The first characteristic to note is that visiting is essentially a group activity: about 90 per cent of visitors are members of a party, the average size of which was 2.7 persons.[4] So it is likely that, typically, several people will be involved in the decision to visit the Museum. Several categories of visitor can be distinguished:

Stayers, whose visit to Beamish was during a period when they spent at least one night away from home, staying in the North-East.

Day trippers, comprise the rest. They may be subdivided into three categories:

Local home-based day trippers, whose home address is in the North-East, who started from and returned to their home address on the day of their visit to Beamish;

Non-local home-based day trippers, whose address is not in the North-East and who started from and returned to their home address on the day of their visit to Beamish;

Other day trippers, who were typically people who did not start or finish at their home address.

This categorization is based on responses to various questions posed during the visitor survey, as shown in Appendix 6. The distribution of visitors is shown in Table 5.1. Ideally, the kind of modelling adopted in Section 5.4 should be applied to each category of visitor separately. Unfortunately data constraints do not permit this. However in the analysis of visitor expenditure in Section 4.4 and Appendix 3 account was taken of differences in the spending patterns (including diverted spending) of the various groups mentioned above.

Visitors to Beamish range across different socioeconomic groups. The visitor survey showed that manual workers are unusually well represented. Amongst the population as a whole the propensity to visit museums is much greater for professional and intermediate occupations than for manual occupations,[5] whereas Table 5.2 shows that, in the case of Beamish, there is almost as great a proportion of

Table 5.1 Percentage distribution of visitor types

Visitor type		Percentage
Stayers		44
Day trippers		56
Local home-based day trippers	29	
Non-local home-based day trippers	17	
Other day trippers	9	
Total		100

Note: Figures may not add exactly because of rounding.

Source: Visitor Survey, 1989.

Table 5.2   Visitors by socioeconomic group (percentage distribution)

	Visitor category		
	Stayers	Day trippers	All
Not economically active	11.6	13.5	12.7
Professional and intermediate	56.2	36.1	45.0
Manual	31.6	50.5	42.1

Note: The respondents were typically the male head of the visiting party. The 'Not economically active' group excludes retired and unemployed respondents, who were asked to give their previous occupation. Currently almost three-quarters (73.2%) of respondents were economically active, mostly in full-time employment.

Source: Visitor Survey, 1989.

manual workers as professional and intermediate; Beamish does not seem to be the preserve of the middle and upper income groups. As noted earlier in this section, the socioeconomic composition of a given flow of visitors is likely to affect both the volume and character of the total spending generated, and this will have implications for employment.

The visitor survey yielded some useful insights on the nature of the visit to Beamish. Perhaps the first point to establish is that, not surprisingly, the Beamish visit was very much part of a leisure activity: 90 per cent or more of day trippers said that 'holiday/ sightseeing/pleasure' was the main reason for their visit to the Beamish area, as Table 5.3, part 1, shows. Stayers were asked a slightly different question – about why they were visiting the North-East, rather than the Beamish area – and a substantial number (28 per cent) gave 'visiting friends/relatives' as the reason. About 64 per cent of stayers classified their visit as 'holiday/sightseeing/pleasure'. The results on the income elasticity of visitor demand, presented in Section 5.4, reflect this leisure characteristic of the visit to Beamish.

The discussion of specification issues in the formal modelling exercise, in Section 5.4.1, notes that owing to data limitations a number of salient variables have been omitted from the time-series analysis. The first of these omitted variables is the role of advertising and marketing. There is little in the form of hard data which can be used to unravel the effects of marketing, but by way of background

Table 5.3 The pattern of visiting

	Day trippers				
	Local home-based	Non-local home-based	Other	Stayers	All
1 Reason for visiting the area[1]					
% 'holiday/sightseeing/pleasure'	89.0	94.8	96.0	63.9	–
% 'visiting friends/relatives'	3.0	1.0	2.0	28.1	–
2 When decision to visit taken					
% today or yesterday	39.0	19.0	26.0	30.3	30.5
% 3–7 days ago	39.6	34.0	24.0	24.1	30.4
% 7 days – 1 month ago	11.6	22.7	8.0	10.0	12.5
% More than 1 month ago	8.5	21.9	34.0	34.1	24.5
3 Inclusive tour[2]					
% on inclusive tour	6.7	42.3	22.0	8.1	–
4 Transport					
% came by car	87.5	45.5	72.0	90.8	80.2
% came by coach	8.5	42.3	20.0	7.2	14.8
% came by train	0.6	10.3	8.0	0.0	2.7
5 Other visits in NE today					
% Yes	15.9	1.0	20.0	–	–
6 Duration of visit (hours)					
Mean	3.93	4.00	3.96	4.12	4.02
Mode	2.75	4.75	3.50	4.00	3.50
7 Previous visits					
% Been before	63.4	17.5	14.0	19.3	31.4
Number of previous visits (mean)	1.62	0.25	0.38	0.38	0.72

1. These items have not been summed because in giving the reason for visiting the area, the day trippers would probably treat 'area' more narrowly than stayers and take the immediate locality of Beamish.
2. These items have not been summed because the inclusive tour was different for day trippers and stayers (the latter being a major trip involving a stay away from home).

Source: Visitor Survey, 1989.

information the visitor survey did yield information on aspects of visitor decision making and behaviour which is relevant to the design of marketing strategies.

An example of such information is the decision to visit Beamish and the mode of transport. The decision to visit the Museum was typically taken within the week prior to the visit (by just over 60 per cent of the survey respondents), though as Table 5.3, part 2 shows, this was most marked for local day trippers (about 80 per cent). Non-local day trippers tended to take the decision to visit Beamish further in advance; this was almost certainly associated with the fact that a comparatively high proportion of them, over 40 per cent, were on an inclusive tour, which would often be planned over a week ahead. This is shown in Table 5.3, part 3. The table also shows, in part 4, correspondingly, that this category of visitor has a much higher likelihood than other visitors of travelling by coach. For most other visitors the normal mode of transport was car.

Another example of information relevant to marketing is the fact that for most day trippers the visit to Beamish was the only 'outing' that day.[6] Not surprisingly, this was the case for virtually all of the non-local day trippers (99 per cent, compared with 80 per cent or more for the rest of day trippers; see Table 5.3, part 5). Time was an obvious constraint on making other visits during the day as the average duration of a Beamish visit was about four hours. Stayers would of course be much more likely to visit other places at some time during their stay in the North-East.

The product which visitors purchase – the Beamish experience – does not encompass the whole of the Museum. During the average four-hour typical visit (see Table 5.3, part 6) not all of the exhibits are visited. Table 5.4 shows that there was very little difference across visitor categories in the exhibits visited. It also suggests that a visit to the Town is a quintessential element in the Beamish experience – almost everyone visited it – but for the other exhibits there were some distinct groupings: the colliery, colliery cottages and station were visited by 85–90 per cent of the visitor survey sample; the farm and transport collection by 70–80 per cent; and the drift mine by about 30 per cent (this low figure may have been partly attributable to capacity constraints rather than lower interest). The catering facilities were used by a minority. It is clear from these data that the mix of components which goes to make up the Beamish experience varies from visitor to visitor.

Table 5.4 *Exhibits visited (percentage in each visitor category visiting the exhibit shown)*

	Day trippers	Stayers	All
Tram	83.3	84.3	83.7
Bus	24.1	26.9	25.4
Town	99.7	99.6	99.6
Colliery	85.9	90.8	88.0
Farm	72.7	77.5	74.8
Station	87.1	90.0	88.4
Colliery cottages	85.9	90.0	87.7
Drift mine	29.9	35.3	32.3
Transport depot	76.5	79.1	77.7
Sun Inn	28.0	22.1	25.4
Tea room	41.8	48.2	44.8

	Day trippers		
	Local home-based	Non-local home-based	Other
Tram	83.5	77.3	94.0
Bus	23.8	20.6	32.0
Town	99.4	100.0	100.0
Colliery	86.6	84.5	86.0
Farm	75.0	90.1	70.0
Station	90.7	82.5	86.0
Colliery cottages	85.4	84.5	90.0
Drift mine	28.7	29.9	34.0
Transport depot	76.2	79.4	72.0
Sun Inn	29.3	27.8	24.0
Tea room	38.4	44.3	48.0

Source: Visitor Survey, 1989.

The fact that not all of the exhibits can be comfortably visited within the span of the average visit means that repeat visits would be necessary to experience all that Beamish has to offer.[7] This has not always been the case: when the Museum was smaller it would have been possible to visit all the exhibits. In more recent years it has been a conscious marketing strategy to make the Beamish experience a changing one, by adding new exhibits or altering existing ones, so that repeat visiting becomes more common. The rate of decay of the experience, which was referred to earlier in this section, will be greater the more the product is changed.

The discussion of specification issues in Section 5.4.1 also comments on the lack of any attempt to model first-time and repeat visits separately, and on the various issues related to the distance travelled by visitors. Again the omission of these factors arises from data limitations. The visitor survey did, however, provide some information, for 1989, on the frequency of visiting and on the geographical origin of visitors. These pieces of information are discussed in the rest of this section: they provide data which, ideally, should be available on a time-series basis for a full modelling exercise.

There are some pronounced variations in the incidence of repeat visits. On average almost a third of all respondents to the visitor survey had been to Beamish before (see Table 5.3, part 7) but the figure was much higher (over 60 per cent) for local day trippers than for all other categories of visitor (less than 20 per cent). This is not surprising in view of the lower cost of time and transport. Table 5.3 shows that in the case of local day trippers the mean number of previous visits was over four times higher than for other groups. This frequency of visiting may explain the comparatively short modal duration of visit for local day trippers shown in Table 5.3, part 6.

The distance travelled by visitors to Beamish is likely to be important in determining not only the frequency of repeat visits but also the price of a 'day out'. Visitors to Beamish are drawn from all parts of the UK. About a third are from the Northern region (2.5 per cent from Cumbria and 30.2 from the North-East) and the rest are distributed as shown in Figure 5.1. The numbers of visitors, as shown for instance by the percentage distribution in each region, are of course influenced by the size of the regional population from which they are drawn. As the note to the figure indicates, allowance has therefore been made for the population differences between regions. The importance of allowing for population can easily be seen, for example, by noting that the South-East, which in absolute terms provided twice as many visitors as the East Midlands (15.7 per cent of total visitors compared with 7.7 per cent), only provided half as many relative to the size of its population. A casual inspection of

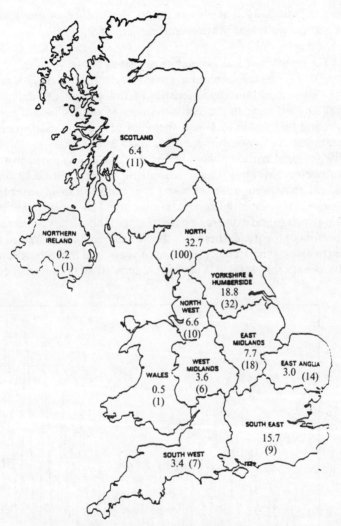

Note: Figures show percentage of survey respondents from each region. Not shown are 2% from the rest of Europe and 1.4% from North America.

Figures in brackets show the number of survey respondents per million population in each region as a percentage of the number of respondents per million population in the northern region.

Source: Visitor Survey, 1989.

Figure 5.1   The origin of visitors to Beamish

Figure 5.1 suggests that distance and the quality of transport networks have a major bearing on the origin of visitors.

5.3   The growth and seasonal nature of visiting

Figure 2.1 charted the substantial growth in visitors in the 1970s and 1980s. Two important characteristics of this growth are that the overall upward trend in the annual number of visitors has not been stable, and that within each year there has been a very marked and regular cycle, as shown in Figures 5.2 and 5.3.

The seasonal pattern shown in Figure 5.3 was computed in the following way. Monthly data were available over the period 1975 to 1978 and these were analysed using the 'ratio to moving average technique'. This involved computing the trend as a twelve-month moving average and expressing particular monthly observations as a proportion of the trend; these monthly ratios were then examined in order to assess their stability in different years, and they were found to be remarkably stable.[8] The figures show that in January, for

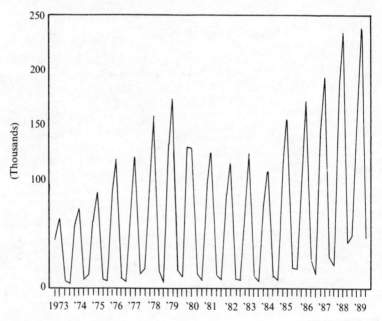

*Figure 5.2   Seasonal pattern of visiting over time (quarterly obser-
vations of the number of visitors)*

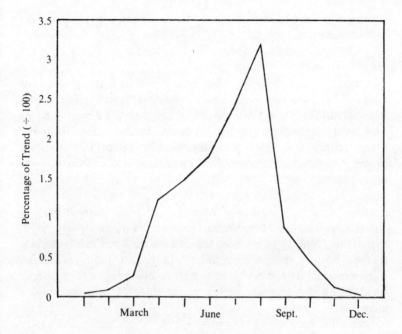

Figure 5.3   Standardized seasonal cycle of visitor flows

example, typical visitor flows are 96 per cent below the trend value, whereas in August they are 220 per cent above the trend. This pattern is not in the least surprising and may be wholly 'explained' by correlating the monthly observations of visitor flows (as a percentage of the twelve-month moving average) with the monthly figures for average maximum temperature, average rainfall, and average sun hours.[9] In short, the weather has an important role to play in any analysis of the annual cycle.

5.4 Modelling visitor flows
In modelling the visitor flows at Beamish the technique of single equation estimation was adopted. Although it could be argued that there is an identification issue and that the quantities (the size of the visitor flows) are influenced by price, and vice versa, this is not relevant in this context since it is reasonable in the case of Beamish to treat the 'supply' as infinitely elastic at the prevailing price which

is chosen by the Museum. Thus a single equation approach is likely to be appropriate.

5.4.1   The model

The model of visitor demand has been based on a straightforward application of the economic theory of demand which indicates that the demand for a good or service will be determined mainly by its own price, by the price of other goods and by consumers' income.[10] These 'economic variables' have therefore been used, in a quarterly model,[11] together with some dummy variables to capture various other effects.

Seasonal, 'quality' and Easter dummies   The use of these dummy variables will be considered first. Three sets of dummies were used. First, it has already been noted that the visitor flows exhibit a clear seasonal pattern: there is great stability in the distribution of visitors over the year. The flows were therefore modelled in a log-linear form, using simple shift dummy variables to capture the seasonality.[12]

Secondly, there is a need to model 'quality' changes as the nature of the Museum's 'product' has changed significantly over the years. In the 1970s, for example, the Museum progressively built up its exhibits: 1973 saw the first public ride on the tram; in 1976 the Victorian bandstand, the temporary visitor centre and Rowley Station were opened; the pit cottages and signal box opened in the following year; and two years later, the drift mine was completed. The *lack* of development at the end of the decade and the beginning of the 1980s almost certainly played some part in the downturn in visitor numbers identified in Figure 2.1. It has not been possible to model these quality changes in any depth. However for two key developments, the opening of the Town Street and the new visitor centre, dummies were introduced to reflect the quality change. The dummies were introduced in a manner which allows there to be a 'decay' in the effect: both dummies take the value one in the period of introduction, but then the dummies each decline so that in the next period they take the value 0.9, 0.8 and so on to a value of 0.1, which is then maintained. This is a rather crude attempt to capture the likely decline of the influence of such quality changes. Finally the timing of Easter is also likely to have an impact, and Easter may fall in either the first or second quarter. Two dummies were introduced to capture the effect, one taking the value one in quarter one if Easter Sunday falls in that quarter and zero otherwise, and a second dummy which takes the value one in quarter two if Easter Sunday falls in that quarter and zero otherwise; this allows there to be a differential impact upon visitor flows, depending upon the quarter in which Easter falls.

'Economic' variables The equation also included the following 'economic' variables. The first was the entry price to Beamish. It can be argued that the relevant price is the cost of the whole outing, and should therefore include travel costs and possibly the cost of meals out (bought either inside or outside the Museum) and other shopping. This again raises questions about the definition of the product demanded, that is, whether it is admission to the Museum or some wider experience, which might include visits to other tourist attractions. In the present context attention has been confined to entry price. This is partly because time-series data on the whole day's spending are hard to obtain,[13] and partly because it is of interest to examine the own-price elasticity of demand. The second 'variable' included was the retail price index (RPI), as a measure of the price of other goods, and the third was disposable personal income.

Specification issues When the equation incorporating these dummies and economic variables was first estimated it showed marked autocorrelation in the residuals which was interpreted as an indicator of mis-specification. Any regression equation is necessarily characterized by errors, omissions and approximations; however, a well-specified equation will have residuals which are consistent with a non-systematic error structure, and the presence of autocorrelation indicates that the error contains some systematic components. This clearly indicates that the specification is deficient in some way, and further analysis is required. The deficiencies may arise, *inter alia*, from the use of an incorrect functional form, a mis-specified set of regressors or data which are inadequate proxies for their theoretical counterparts.

In a simple equation which seeks to explain visitor flows by a set of dummies (thought *a priori* to be important and which have theoretical justification) and a set of contemporaneous economic variables, it must be recognized that a number of salient variables may have been omitted or may have been mis-specified. One obvious variable which has been omitted is the role of advertising and marketing. The exclusion is because of the absence of suitable data.[14] It would be strange to suppose that marketing behaviour had no effect on visitor flows, but it is not possible to do more than make casual observations, for example that the number of visitors rose in the mid-1980s following a new commitment to the marketing of the Museum in the face of falling visitor flows in the early 1980s. Crucially one would need a variable which captured the marketing effort[15] relative to that of other competing attractions. Without such a measure it is best to proceed without the variable – it is inappropriate to use an invalid proxy – and exercise due judgement in interpreting the results with marketing omitted.

A second potentially important omission is direct recognition of the effect of information 'trickling down' through the potential population of visitors. Visitors tell others of Beamish and this leads to increased demand as awareness of the Museum becomes more widespread. There is, however, some attempt to capture some aspects of this process by the use of the lagged dependent variable as described below.

Thirdly, there is no attempt to model the composition of demand in terms of first-time and repeat visits. The frequency of visits is likely to depend, as noted in Section 5.2, on such factors as the distance from the Museum and the rate of decay of the initial experience.

A closely allied point is that there is no explicit recognition of the fact that as the local demand becomes saturated continued growth in demand generally entails drawing visitors from more and more distant locations. Travel costs rise and the price of a 'day out' (rather than simply the admission price) increases *pari passu*. There may be several complex interactions. It was noted earlier, for example, that repeat visits are more likely for visitors who live nearer, and the attraction's marketing strategies may influence and be influenced by the geographical source of visitors. In the absence of suitable data no attempt has been made to model these aspects in our time-series analysis.[16]

Finally, possible supply constraints and the role of competitors have not been examined.

The model does, however, acknowledge some of the subtleties in the consumption decisions. Individuals may, for example, react to *previous* values of the admission price, of their own disposable income and of the general price level; specifically, the rate of change of the admission price may be salient, as may the rate of growth of their income, and the rate of growth of RPI may also be important. In order to examine these possibilities, the original specification was expanded to include the lagged values of the entry price, of disposable income, of RPI and of visitor flows as additional explanatory variables. The inclusion of the lagged dependent variable allows for the 'trickle-down' effect referred to earlier and for habit persistence: see for example, Witt (1980) and Witt and Martin (1987b). The latter effect implies that individuals will make repeat visits: *ceteris paribus*, an individual who has made a visit in period t, is more likely to do so in period t + 1.

The form of the estimated equation Thus the equation to be estimated included, in addition to the dummies previously described, current and previous values of price, disposable income and the general price level, and a lagged dependent variable. This resulted in a well-specified regression equation which successfully passed the key diagnostic tests.

In fact the estimated equation may be written in a somewhat simplified form: starting with a general equation whose specification is determined by theoretical considerations a number of data-based simplifications can be made.[17] Specifically, it turns out that the coefficients on the current and lagged entry price are not significantly different in size, but are of opposite sign, and this allows the combination of the two independent variables of current and lagged price in difference form. Also, it is possible to combine the disposable income variables with the general price level and write the equation in terms of current deflated disposable income, and its rate of growth.

5.4.2 The results
Using these simplifications the equation, which was estimated over the period 1975, second quarter, to 1988, third quarter, may then be written in the following terms.

$$\ln(V) =$$
$$-13.53 + 0.64Q_1 + 3.20Q_2 + 2.71Q_3 + 0.91E_1 + 0.69E_2$$
$$(4.65) \quad (0.28) \quad (0.29) \quad (0.09) \quad (0.14) \quad (0.16)$$

$$+0.08X_1 + 0.22X_2 - 0.91S - 0.54\ln(P/P_{-1}) + 3.10\ln(rpdi)$$
$$(0.11) \quad (0.13) \quad (0.18) \quad (0.17) \quad (0.90)$$

$$+1.21\ln(rpdi/rpdi_{-1}) - 0.55\ln(RPI) + 0.45\ln V_{-1}$$
$$(1.27) \quad (0.17) \quad (0.11)$$

(Standard errors are in parentheses)
R-Squared = 0.9880; F-Statistic [F(13,40)] = 253.0602
R-Bar-Squared = 0.9841; S.E. of Regression = 0.1641
DW-statistic = 1.7834; Durbin's h-statistic = 1.3412
where V = the visitor flow
         Q_i = 1 in quarter 1, 0 otherwise
         E_i = 1 if Easter Sunday falls in quarter i, 0 otherwise
         X_1 = product quality dummy: Town Street, see text
         X_2 = product quality dummy; visitor centre, see text
         S = exceptional weather dummy (see text and note 18):
                1 in 1979 Q1, 0 otherwise
         P = the full admission price (average for the quarter)
     rpdi = real personal disposable income
     RPI = Retail Price Index

Diagnostic tests are reported in Appendix 7.

It is important to note that the lagged variables, although included in a general way, may be written in the specific form as above. The estimated equation allows the current and lagged admission price to be written as the logarithm of the ratio of current to last period's price; this is (approximately) the percentage increase in the admission price and, as expected, has a significant negative sign. The estimated equation also indicates that the role of the general price level is felt through the variable 'rpdi' which is nominal personal disposable income deflated by the RPI, and through the logarithm of the ratio of current to last period's 'real' personal disposable income (which is, approximately, the percentage rate of growth of 'real' personal disposable income), and also through the term in the RPI itself. Furthermore, the last period's visitor flows have a significant positive effect on the current flows. This latter variable may be explained by reference to the role of potentially important, though immeasurable, variables: as information on the Museum percolates through the potential visitor population this increases visitor flows further, many visitors repeat their visits, and direct advertising (such as that through car stickers displayed by previous visitors) also acts to increase the number of visitors. This lagged flow variable may be interpreted as catching the aggregation of such effects.

The estimated equation performs as predicted by theory: the role of admission prices is significant and negative, and the current demand for admission would appear to be price inelastic (a 1 per cent rise in the current admission prices appears to reduce current demand by about a half of 1 per cent, *ceteris paribus*). The influence of current 'real' personal disposable income is significant and positive, and indicates a relatively large short-run elasticity of 4.31; however, not only does the level of income matter, but so does the direction of growth: growth in income increases demand. (This coefficient on the growth of rpdi is not well defined, but its deletion produces autocorrelation in the residuals, indicating that excluding this variable results in some mis-specification, and on this criterion its inclusion is justified.) The general price level has a further role to play, in addition to deflating nominal incomes: even if incomes and prices were to rise in the same proportion this equation indicates that demand for museum admission would fall. This suggests that, even if real incomes were maintained, general inflation results in consumers switching demand away from such leisure activities as museums. The role of the last period's visitor numbers is, as predicted, significant and positive, and this must be interpreted as catching a large number of omitted, non-measurable, influences. The signs and significance of the coefficients on own price, income and the lagged dependent variable are in line with results from the aggregate studies of tourism flows: see, for example, Witt and Martin (1985).

The estimated equation also indicates that the quarterly effects are all significant, as is to be expected, and the quality changes both have positive impacts, though the coefficient on the Town Street dummy is not well defined. The effect of Easter is positive, and significant, with the size of the impact depending upon the quarter in which Easter falls. (The dummy variable S takes account of the exceptionally bad weather of quarter one, 1979, during which the North-East suffered greatly from snow conditions.)[18]

5.5. Summary

The flow of visitors is a major determinant of the employment impact of the Museum, and is also likely to have a bearing on local authority funding, and the employment financed by such funding. A detailed examination of visitors is warranted, so this chapter has described the characteristics of visitors and some aspects of their behaviour, and has presented a quarterly econometric model of visitor flows.

Visiting Beamish is a leisure activity which is typically engaged in by groups rather than individuals. The visitors are drawn from a wide range of socioeconomic groups and it seems less elitist than some other museums in the social composition of its visitors. For most visitors, the trip to the Museum comprises 'a day out': typically they do not visit other places. Whilst at the Museum, however, they do not visit all the exhibits during the four hours which on average they spend there. The product – the visitor experience – has changed over the years by the provision of additional facilities and this has accelerated the rate of decay of the experience. The changing product has been accompanied by more repeat visits especially amongst local visitors (of whom 63 per cent are repeat visitors). Visitors to Beamish are drawn from all over the UK: about 70 per cent are from outside the North-East.

Since its opening in 1972 visitor numbers have grown substantially, though unevenly, to a level of almost half a million in 1989. There is a very pronounced seasonal pattern in visiting, which seems to be almost entirely weather-dependent.

An econometric model of visitor flows has been developed. The single equation model used is subject to a number of limitations, which have been discussed, but it nevertheless provides some clear results which are of interest both as a test of economic theory and as a potentially useful management tool which may be applicable, *mutatis mutandis*, to other individual attractions.

The model shows the relevance of admission prices and of real personal disposable income as determinants of demand. In the short run, price elasticity over the range experienced is low (about -0.5) and income elasticity is high (about $+4.3$). These results are robust and suggest that a simple model of this kind can provide insights into the determinants of visitor flows. This is not to deny that more sophisticated modelling, taking account of some of the issues raised in this chapter, would not be desirable.[19]

The strength of the estimated equation permits a measure of confidence that the model may be of some value in aiding the formation of managerial judgements, for example about the size of the elasticities and about future visitor flows. Other findings are also potentially significant. The remarkable stability in the distribution of demand across the four quarters suggests, for instance, that it might be difficult to alter this pattern. Thus redistributing the summer peak might be possible but is likely to require substantial effort. The role of certain product developments and the carry-over effects from one period to the next are also highlighted.

Notes

1. This is of course a particular manifestation of the general issue of whether tourism is essentially self-destructive in so far as success, in terms of increased numbers of tourists, often tends to damage the very things it is seeking.
2. Considerable research attention has been given to the formal econometric modelling of tourism demand between countries in recent years. For a brief review of these studies, see Ashworth and Johnson (1990) and Johnson and Ashworth (1990). The study described in this chapter complements these 'macro' studies by formally modelling demand at the level of the individual tourist attraction.
3. Decisions on pricing, investment, staffing, marketing and product development are, for example, likely to be affected by their implications for demand; moreover some of these decisions will be a consequence of past or forecast trends in demand. While the formal modelling of demand cannot be a substitute for the intimate, intuitive knowledge of visitor flows that managers may have built up over many years – frequently, an econometric analysis cannot easily capture some of the more 'qualitative' factors which managers may think are important – it can nevertheless provide an appropriate base from which to work. It is thus a useful complement to managerial intuition and an aid to judgement.
4. The average party size differed very little across visitor categories.
5. Evidence from the General Household Survey 1986 (reported in *Social Trends 20*, 1990 edition, Table 10.3) shows that the following percentage in each group visited a museum/art gallery in the four weeks before interview

Professional, employers and managers	6
Intermediate and junior non-manual	5
Skilled manual	2
Semi-skilled and unskilled manual	2

6. The most commonly mentioned places for other visits were Durham City (7 per cent of all visitors), the coast (2 per cent) and the Metro Centre shopping complex at Gateshead (2 per cent).
7. An alternative would be to lengthen the present duration of visits, though it seems unlikely that there is much scope for this. It is interesting to note that in the case of some museums, such as Ironbridge, the way to get most out of the museum (in the eyes of its Director) is to spread the visit over two or three consecutive days.
8. The fact that there has been great stability in the past does not mean that the

pattern is immutable and that there is no scope for altering the pattern, for example by more pronounced differential pricing.

9. For each weather variable, the overall average and the average for each of the twelve months was computed, and a new variable was created comprising the average monthly observation as a ratio to its overall average. Now using the twelve observations and regressing the natural logarithm of the visitor flow ratio (described in the text) to a constant, and natural logarithms of the three weather variables in ratio form, yields the following:

$$\ln(\text{vis}) = -0.52 + 1.19 \ln(\text{temp}) + 2.20 \ln(\text{sun}) - 0.79 \ln(\text{rain})$$
$$\quad\quad (0.08)\quad (0.38)\quad\quad\quad (0.38)\quad\quad\quad (0.43)$$
R-Squared: 0.98

The results of the diagnostic tests were as follows:

Serial correlation: 2.34 (5% critical value: 3.84)
Functional form: 0.01 (5% critical value: 3.84)
Normality: 2.19 (5% critical value: 5.99)
Heteroscedasticity: 0.90 (5% critical value: 3.84)

Clearly, the regression accounts for almost all the variation on the monthly cycle (98 per cent of the variation is explained), and the regression passes all diagnostic tests.

10. The variables own price, income, and prices of other goods and services appear (in one form or another) in the 'macro' studies of tourism referred to in note 2, although the precise specification of each variable varies. See, for example, Martin and Witt (1988) for a discussion of alternative methods including substitute prices.
11. The decision to use a quarterly model was governed by availability of data for the independent variables.
12. The log-linear form has been widely used in studies of tourism demand: see, for example, Witt and Martin (1987a) and the studies quoted therein.
13. The visitor survey (see Appendix 5) yielded information on such spending only for a particular point in time.
14. Most 'macro' studies of tourism do not include an advertising or marketing variable. For an exception see Papadopoulos and Witt (1985). Again the data requirements for an advertising/marketing variable are quite severe since the advertising/market efforts of *competing* countries should also be included if the model is to be correctly specified.
15. The form of marketing may be as important as the level of expenditure.
16. Travel costs are usually incorporated as an explanatory variable in studies modelling tourist movement between countries (see Johnson and Ashworth, 1990), and they have been used in studies of the visitor demand for particular attractions (see Morgan, 1986). Witt (1980) also includes a travel *time* variable in his analysis of overseas tourism by UK residents.
17. The entry price (P), real personal disposable income (rpdi) and general price index terms (RPI) in the estimated equation were derived as follows. Denoting Y as nominal personal disposable income the contribution of P, Y and RPI may be specified by:

$$-\beta\ln(P) + \beta_1\ln(P_1) + \delta\ln(Y) - \delta_1\ln(Y_1) - \pi\ln(RPI) + \pi_{-1}\ln(RPI_{-1})$$

This may be written as:

$$- \beta\ln(P/P_{-1}) - (\beta - \beta_{-1})\ln(P_{-1}) + \delta\ln(Y/RPI) - \delta_{-1}\ln(Y_{-1}/RPI_{-1}) - (\pi - \delta)\ln(RPI) + (\pi_{-1} - \delta_{-1})\ln(RPI_{-1})$$

The hypothesis that $\beta = \beta_{-1}$ could be rejected and so the separate term in P_{-1} is redundant; equally, the hypothesis that $\pi_{-1} - \delta_{-1} = 0$ could not be rejected and so the separate term in RPI_{-1} is also redundant. Thus the equation may be written as:

$$- \beta\ln(P/P_{-1}) + \delta\ln(rpdi) - \delta_{-1}\ln(rpdi_{-1}) - (\pi - \delta)\ln(RPI)$$

This may now be written as

$$- \beta\ln(P/P_{-1}) + (\delta - \delta_{-1})\ln(rpdi) + \delta_{-1}\ln(rpdi/rpdi_{-1}) - (\pi - \delta)\ln(RPI)$$

and this is the form of the equation reported in the text.

18. In the first quarter of 1979 there were 22 days in January with one or more inches of snow lying at 9.00 a.m., 12 such days in February, and 13 such days in March. This was far greater than for any other year since the early 1960s.

19. For example, the possibility of there being some ceiling to the growth of visitor numbers might be considered but in fact, in this case study, the fit of a log-linear model to the sample data is extremely good and experiments with variable elasticities did not perform well.

6 Employment potential[1]

6.1 Introduction

This chapter examines some of the determinants of the Museum's future employment impact. The underlying question is: what are the key influences on the Museum's employment potential? Section 6.2 takes a longer-term view and briefly examines the evidence on whether or not a product life cycle exists among open-air museums. The existence of such a cycle clearly has important implications for employment and for management strategy. In Section 6.3 the ways in which management action can affect employment in the shorter term are examined. The final section looks at the relationship between the Museum's employment and public policy.

Some of the discussion in this chapter draws on comparisons between Beamish and other open-air museums operating in the UK and elsewhere (Johnson and Thomas, 1990b). Appendix 8 outlines the basis on which these other museums were selected and provides some summary information on each.

6.2 The longer-term view: is there a product life cycle?

It has already been argued that the Museum's employment is affected positively by visitor numbers. Chapter 5 offered some insights into the factors that influence those numbers. What that chapter was unable to do was to offer any comparisons between trends in visitor flows at Beamish and those at other museums. Yet such comparisons can provide some, albeit crude, guide to the competitiveness of Beamish and the experience it offers, and hence to likely future trends in employment. In this section some comparative data on visitor flows are presented.

For each open-air museum included in the comparisons described in Appendix 8, data on visitor numbers were collected for recent years. Before looking at these data, it is important to recognize some limitations surrounding the use of visitor numbers. First, and most obviously, visitor numbers are affected by a range of variables – some of which were considered in Chapter 5 – and not simply by the experience on offer. Secondly, as Appendix 8 shows, there are variations in the activities to which the visitor numbers relate. Although

84

all the museums considered here have core open-air sections, they also embrace a variety of other activities, the existence of which inevitably affects visitor numbers. The 'noise' in the data as far as open-air activities are concerned must be acknowledged when interpreting the visitor numbers. Thirdly, how visitor numbers are actually counted must also be taken into account. Counting procedures usually depend on how visitors pay admission. (Appendix 8 gives an example of how these procedures can affect the visitor count.)

Finally, visitor numbers may provide little guide to what is happening to the financial position of the museum. Rapid growth of visitor numbers is, for example, quite compatible with falling profitability; a *reduction* in visitor numbers brought about by raising prices may raise profitability.

In Figure 6.1 trends in visitor numbers in each of the museums during the 1980s are shown. The 1980s represent different stages of development in each of the museums. The Black Country Museum for example is still a comparative youngster whereas Skansen has been in operation for nearly a century. (The latter had already reached 2 million visitors per year by 1938.) All the Scandinavian museums have had generally static or declining visitor numbers. At certain times the fall has been particularly substantial; for example, numbers visiting Skansen fell by nearly 20 per cent between 1983 and 1987 (although there was a slight recovery in 1988). In the Netherlands, the Zuiderzee Museum has declined continuously since opening in 1983. Visitor numbers at Arnhem have shown a more erratic picture, although once the exceptional figures for 1987 – generated by the public reaction to a government proposal to close the museum – are discounted, the trend has been static after falling in the early 1980s.

In the UK, the Ulster Folk and Transport and Welsh Folk Museums have shown no significant growth over the period, whereas both Beamish and the Black Country Museum have displayed a strong upward trend. (Beamish did, however, experience a decline up to 1984: see Chapter 2.) Ironbridge showed only modest growth in the first half of the 1980s, but grew very rapidly between 1987 and 1988.

The recent growth of Beamish, the Black Country Museum and Ironbridge, and the relative stagnation or decline of the other museums have in part reflected differences in the kind of museum

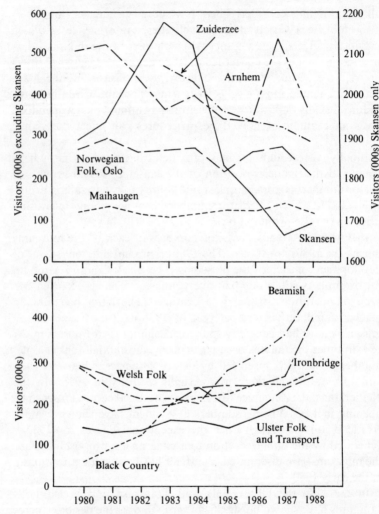

Note: The Maihaugen figures relate to admission-paying visitors only. The Ulster Folk and Transport Museum numbers include visitors to the Transport Museum and the Witham Street Collection. The numbers for Ironbridge relate to individuals who purchase tickets (see Appendix 8). These numbers are of course considerably less than those relating to site visits. Those for the other museums include visitors to the indoor galleries and exhibitions. The data on which this Figure is based were obtained in interviews with the staff of each museum.

Figure 6.1   Visitor numbers, 1980–8: selected open-air museums

experience that has been offered. The Scandinavian, Arnhem, Welsh Folk and Ulster Folk and Transport Museums are all in (what may be termed) the European folk museum tradition (Brown, 1986), where the emphasis has been primarily on the buildings and on the artefacts associated with them. To date, rural life has been the traditional focus although that emphasis is now beginning to change: for example the Ulster Folk and Transport Museum is now developing an urban area. Craft demonstrations are important, but the number of 'working' exhibits is relatively small. (The Zuiderzee Museum does not fit easily into this group. It is very much concerned with village/town life, although the emphasis until recently has been on the buildings and exhibits themselves rather than on the life associated with them.) In contrast the three high-growth museums belong to a rather different, more modern tradition, focusing on urban and industrial life and providing a range of activities and working exhibits that goes beyond craft demonstrations.

The no growth/declining museums have sought to adapt. For example, the Welsh Folk Museum was subject to an extensive review in 1985–6 (Brown, 1986), a review which recommended that the museum's remit should be broadened beyond its traditional 'folk' image (see the National Museum of Wales' *Annual Report* 1987–88, p.21). The Arnhem Museum has also sought to move away from its traditional focus on pre-industrial rural life (de Jong, 1988) and Maihaugen is now doing so (Valen-Sendstad, 1986). Mention has already been made of the Ulster Folk and Transport Museum's urban development. Of course resource and other constraints may mean that the pace of change is suboptimal and/or slower than management and/or funding bodies would wish.

Although the data on visitor numbers must be treated cautiously, for the reasons given earlier, they do nevertheless suggest some form of product life cycle for open-air museums: the old folk/rural tradition – epitomized by the Scandinavian museums – no longer has the attraction it once had, whereas the generally newer urban/ industrial group which tends also to have a greater emphasis on working demonstrations has experienced expansion in visitor numbers. This conclusion is borne out by Figure 6.2, which relates the age of each museum to the growth in its visitor numbers since 1980.[2] It clearly indicates two clusters of visitor growth rates.[3] It is worth noting that the newer urban/industrial product has been developed via new museums rather than by the older museums

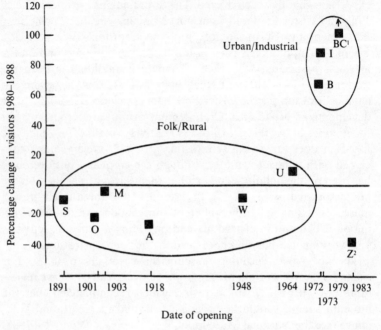

Figure 6.2   Visitor trends and types of open-air museum

Legend
S   Skansen   U   Ulster Folk and Transport
O   Oslo (Norwegian Folk)   Z   Zuiderzee
M   Maihaugen   B   Beamish
A   Arnhem   BC   Black Country
W   Welsh Folk   I   Ironbridge

Notes: The data on which this Figure is based were obtained in interviews with staff of each musum.
1. The Black Country Museum experienced a growth rate of 371 per cent.
2. The Zuiderzee Museum's visitors cover the period 1983–8. It is very much an outlier in terms of its date of opening but it had an unusually long gestation period. The present site was selected in 1932, the first grant for construction was in 1946, and construction began in 1963. If one of these earlier dates had been plotted instead of its official opening, it would 'conform' to the folk/rural pattern.

changing from their traditional rural product. This is in line with evidence from manufacturing industry (see for example Jewkes *et al.*, 1969) which shows that new rather than established organizations have long been an important source of new products and processes. One reason for this is that managements of long-established organizations sometimes tend to get locked in to the products they produce and the markets they serve.

Figures 6.1 and 6.2 are based on only a few years, and do not relate open-air museums *as a group* to other groups of museums or to other types of tourist attraction. Nevertheless they reinforce the warning given at the end of Chapter 2 that to sustain visitor demand, and hence employment, the experience offered by Beamish and by the newer museums in general must remain under constant review and development. As Beamish found at the beginning of the 1980s, when its visitor numbers fell (see Figure 2.1) partly (although not wholly) as the result of the absence of new developments, no museum product – however good when first introduced – has an inbuilt perpetual competitive advantage.

6.3 The role of management

6.3.1 The scope for management action

The possibility that the experience offered by a museum such as Beamish follows a product life cycle has obvious implications for management. Clearly employment will only be maintained in the longer term if the management is able to counter the effects of any such cycle by major product innovation. Such innovation may even lead to an *increase* in employment.

In this section the focus moves away from the longer term. It considers how management might be able to change the employment impact of the Museum over a shorter time horizon with the broad nature of the experience on offer being taken as given. (Some lower-order quality changes may still be made.) The taxonomy of employment types created by the existence of Beamish which were depicted in Figure 4.1 may be used here as a basis for discussion. It should be noted at the outset that some of these types of employment are more easily affected by management action than others. For example employment in Beamish itself is most directly affected by management behaviour whereas the latter may exercise little influence over the scale of induced employment arising from any given level of Museum activity.

Whether or not management initiates action which will raise employment will depend crucially on the objectives of decision takers and the constraints under which they operate. More will be said about objectives in Section 6.3.2.

Constraints may be of many types, including those of a financial, political and planning character. As Chapter 5 has shown, general economic conditions over which the Museum has little control, also have an important influence on visitor demand and hence on employment: for example, demand is highly sensitive to incomes. The rate at which incomes grow, and the volatility of such growth, must be taken largely as given by the Museum's management, although it may be able to exercise some influence over the *sensitivity* of visitor demand to incomes. As Chapter 3 showed, a volatile growth record may make management cautious about taking on too many permanent staff, because such a strategy reduces its room for manoeuvre in the event of a downturn.

A further constraint arises from the highly seasonal nature of visitor numbers flows (see Figure 5.2). It may be possible to reduce this seasonality, for example by provision of covered display areas, such as arcades, but given weather patterns, the scope for such levelling out is likely to be limited. Indeed, as argued later, an *accentuation* of seasonal variations in visitor numbers may be the appropriate outcome if the Museum is seeking to increase admission revenues. The seasonal pattern of demand is likely to exercise a considerable influence on the nature of the workforce and the employment contracts offered.

It is always possible to increase employment by lowering technical efficiency, for example by employing two workers to undertake a task for which only one is required. Throughout this chapter, however, it is assumed that this option is not adopted.

Table 4.1 showed that 72 per cent of gross employment was accounted for by direct activities, that is the Museum and associated activity. The division between the Museum's employment and that generated outside the Museum in associated activities is not a hard and fast one. As indicated later, one possible option for the expansion of the Museum is further diversification into catering and retailing operations and indeed into other activities. Colonial Williamsburg in Virginia[4] – which attracts twice as many visitors as Beamish – owns several hotels and is now planning a golf course. In terms of the framework given in Figure 4.1, such a policy would transfer employment from the associated activities heading to the key activity heading. For the moment, however, the breakdown between these activities at Beamish is taken as given.

6.3.2   Direct employment in the Museum (the key activity)

Museum objectives and employment   The maximization of employment has never been a primary objective of the management of Beamish although, as Chapter 1 noted, potential economic benefits were stressed in the early promotional literature for the Museum. Yet increased employment may arise as a consequence of the pursuit of other objectives. For example, if, with a given number of visitors, management aims (and has the resources) to raise the average quality of visitor experience, then an increase in employment is likely. This would also be the case if, for a given average quality of visitor experience, management aims to increase the number of visitors. The precise nature of such an increase – in respect, for example, of the types of jobs created – will depend on how the strategy is affected. For example, the quality of experience may be improved in a variety of ways (more artefacts, more interpretations, better displays, better toilets and catering facilities, and so on). Each method will have different implications for employment, in terms of both its structure and the total numbers involved.

Sources of funds   Additional employment in the Museum has to be financed, so it is important to consider the main sources of funds, of which there are three. The first may be labelled 'commercial'. Such funds derive from catering operations and admission charges. Funding from this source is affected by the objectives pursued by managers, and how they view the nature of the Museum experience.

Figure 6.3 may help to illustrate some of the issues. D_1 is the visitor demand schedule faced by a museum when the (constant) marginal cost for the experience on offer is C_1. Marginal cost pricing yields an admission charge of A_1 and visitor numbers of V_1. The museum may decide to enhance the quality of the experience by raising costs to C_2. This in turn shifts the demand curve out to D_2. Marginal cost pricing at A_2 yields visitor numbers of V_2. In the particular case illustrated in Figure 6.3, $V_2 > V_1$ but it would not be difficult to envisage a result in which $V_1 > V_2$. What happens to employment will depend on the change in visitor numbers and any change in the labour intensity of the experiences offered. ('Better' experiences in a museum context will often imply greater labour intensity.)

A second source of funds for the Museum is the public sector, which for current purposes may be taken as including local

Admission charge/
cost per unit

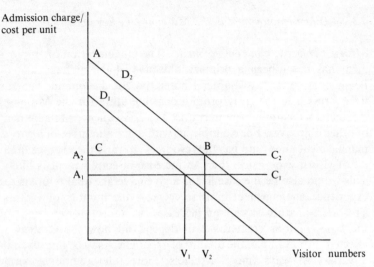

V₁ V₂   Visitor numbers

Figure 6.3   Demand, costs and quality changes

authority, central government (including quasi-governmental organizations such as English Heritage) and European Community
sources. These funds are used for different purposes. Most local
authority funding is for general-purpose revenue expenditure; other
public funds are usually earmarked for specific capital purposes.
There is no reason why the employment expenditure ratios should
be the same across different purposes. The third funding source is
donations from private sources: private foundations, individuals
and companies.

Table 6.1 provides details of the main sources of income on both
revenue and capital account. It is important to note that the precise
breakdown of funding varies from year to year. It should also be
noted that what is defined as 'income' in the table varies from source
to source. Sales less purchases have been used for retailing and
catering since it is this sum that probably comes closest to the
admission income figure. The 'income' on capital account, however,
is the total figure for expenditure (on everything) financed in 1989–
90.

The scope for increasing funding from each of these sources is
considered below. It is over commercial funding (from admissions
and retailing and catering) that the Museum probably has the
greater influence. This source is therefore considered first.

Table 6.1   Sources of income for Beamish, 1989–90

	£(000s)	% of total
Revenue account		
Admission income	1 252.2	48.6
Contribution from local authorities	337.4	13.1
Retailing sales less purchases[1]	266.0	10.3
Catering sales less purchases[2]	188.6	7.3
Other income[3]	222.0	8.6
Total, revenue account	2 266.2	(87.9)
Capital account		
Local authority contributions	174.0	6.7
Borrowing via local authorities	82.9	3.2
Use of Museum's balances and other contributions	54.7	2.1
Development Trust	0.0	0.0
Total, capital account	311.6	(12.1)
Total, revenue and capital accounts	2 577.8	100.0

1. This figure is made up of employee costs (£76.7), running expenses (£12.6) and surplus (£176.7).
2. Catering is now run by the Museum as a contracted out facility. The figure is made up of employee costs (£70.2), the concession payment to the Museum (£90.1), running expenses (£18.0) and surplus (£10.3).
3. This figure includes interest received (£125.0) and miscellaneous income (£97.0).

Source: Beamish accounts.

Admission income   The Museum faces two options over the raising of admission income: it may seek (for a given admission price) to raise visitor numbers, and/or it may raise admission prices. Each option is considered in turn below.

INCREASING VISITOR NUMBERS   An important issue here is the extent to which the Museum's activities are capacity constrained. The concept of 'capacity' for Beamish is not easily defined, partly because the unit of output may vary with visitor numbers – exhibits can always be seen more quickly – and partly because not all visitors may wish to see all the exhibits anyway. Some of these issues are addressed in Darnell *et al.* (1989), which also shows how different exhibits and facilities at Beamish have different throughput capacities (where the latter are defined in terms of what may be 'comfortably' achieved). Despite these problems, it is probably fair to say that apart from a few days in the year in the peak season, the Museum's capacity is not overstretched.[5] The following discussion assumes that any additional visitors generated by management action can be accommodated.

Stimulating visitors who would not otherwise make such a visit to do so, and encouraging a higher *frequency* of repeat visits among those who have already returned or intend to return to the Museum raises a number of important issues for the Museum's management. In particular the latter needs to know how rapidly the visitor experience 'decays' following a visit and how changes in the experience offered affect the rate of decay and the extent of repeat visiting. *Ceteris paribus*, the lower the level of change in the visitor experience the lower the frequency of repeat visits.

Increasing the number of 'virgin' visitors will usually entail drawing visitors from more distant locations, thus increasing the transport costs, and hence the overall price of a visit to Beamish. Marketing costs may also rise. The demographic characteristics of the immediate catchment area will also influence the extent to which new visitors can be attracted from that area. It is likely to be increasingly difficult, for a given museum experience, to generate further new demand from an ageing, static population than from a population characterized by a high birth rate and/or extensive inward flows.

RAISING ADMISSION PRICES   The evidence in Chapter 5 suggests that the price elasticity of visitor demand is substantially less than one. Hence total admission income could be increased by raising prices. Such a policy might, however, reduce access below an acceptable level as far as the local authorities are concerned. It might also lead to some compensating transfer of spending away from the retailing and catering operations of the museum, although there is no direct evidence on this score.

Price increases would almost certainly not have to be confined to the peak period. Indeed visitor demand during the off-peak may be *more* price inelastic. Again there is no direct evidence on this issue, but survey evidence (Johnson and Thomas, 1990a) shows that there is a much higher proportion of professional visitors, and a much lower proportion of unskilled manual visitors in the off-peak period compared with the peak period; the typically higher average incomes that such a change in the mix of visitors generates may imply lower price elasticities.

Greater price discrimination in either or both the peak and off-peak periods, if successfully achieved, would raise admission revenues. But while some discrimination is possible, and is to some extent already practised (for example through lower prices for senior citizens), it is unlikely that it could be greatly extended, because of the difficulty of identifying different groups of visitors, and the alienation that differential charging would bring.

Retailing and catering It is difficult to assess the potential for increasing revenues from retailing and catering. The visitor survey (Appendix 5) did, however, provide some indication of how far revenues per visitor might be raised by generating sales from visitors who do not currently spend anything in the Museum, and/or by increasing the average expenditure of those visitors who already spend. These sources of potential spending may sometimes be very significant. Some estimates are provided in Johnson and Thomas (1990a). For example, the percentage increase in total sales that would result if all 'non-spenders' were to spend the average of the spenders would be 25 per cent. Furthermore, the 'loss' in spending at the Museum that results from overcrowding and/or a product range that does not fully match visitors' preferences could be as much as 35 per cent of annual sales. It is important to stress that these percentages offer no guidance on whether strategies which might tap these sources of potential spending would be commercially viable. They simply identify possibilities that could be explored.

From the international comparisons made in this study, it is clear that Beamish is relatively successful in generating trade from retailing and catering. Table 6.2 shows that the spend per visitor at Beamish is relatively high. The average expenditure figures in the table include, where possible, franchise operations. Except where stated, VAT is excluded. The Beamish figure is exceeded only by Ironbridge, which is able to sell high unit value china items through its Coalport China Works Museum. Catering sales per visitor at Beamish are in line with those elsewhere; if anything they are slightly on the high side. These figures have been achieved despite the fact that Beamish had the highest adult admission charge during the period.

Table 6.2 Sales per visitor

	Financial year ending	Retail sales per visitor (£)	Catering sales per visitor (£)
Beamish	31.3.89	1.32	0.70[1]
Black Country	31.3.89	0.98[2]	0.65
Ironbridge	31.3.89	2.09	0.64
Ulster Folk and Transport	31.3.89	0.46	0.40
Welsh Folk	31.12.89	0.64	n.a.
Arnhem	31.12.88	n.a.	1.43
Zuiderzee	31.12.88	0.59[3]	0.93[3]
Skansen	31.12.88	0.33	n.a.
Maihaugen	31.12.88	0.81	0.75
Norwegian Folk (Oslo)	31.12.88	0.54	n.a.

Notes: The data on which Table 6.2 is based were obtained in interviews with staff of each museum.
1. Includes an estimate for franchised ice-cream sales and the public house.
2. Includes an estimate for sales from the franchised glass cutter, craft workshop and photographer.
3. Includes VAT.

Public funding Management strategies are bound to have some influence on the availability of public funding. The types of project planned, management's ability successfully to attract finance and to monitor its use, and its willingness to accept the various conditions attached to different funds all influence the employment derived from public funds. Beamish has had significant success in attracting funds from a variety of sources (Johnson and Thomas, 1989c). It is doubtful, given its current resources, the nature of its activities, and current policy towards museums, whether substantially greater funding could be attracted. It is nevertheless important that current funding patterns for museums should be examined (see below).

Private donations Over the years, a number of initiatives have been taken to raise funds from private sources, from both individuals and companies. However, the amounts raised have been relatively small. For example, Table 6.1 shows that the Development Trust, which was intended to be a focus for private donations to the Museum, contributed nothing to the capital programme in 1989–90.

It is unclear how much more can be raised from this source; the other museums included in Appendix 8 do not have extensive private funding. On the other hand, in the USA the tradition is different and substantial private funding is much more in evidence. For example at Colonial Williamsburg, gifts and grants amounted in 1989 to nearly 35 per cent of the income derived from admission income.[6] For the Plimoth Plantation in Massachusetts, an altogether smaller operation, the percentage is nearer 10 per cent,[7] still very much higher than that for Beamish. There may be some scope for developing this source of funding. Certainly US museum managements tend to put considerable resources and marketing effort into attracting and then keeping the patronage of private donors.

In considering the scope for increased private donations, it is helpful to consider what private benefits may derive from the Museum which may not be expressed through admission revenues. First, visitors may obtain some consumers' surplus from their visit. For any individual, the consumer's surplus is defined as the difference between what that individual is willing to pay and the amount he/she actually does pay. Figure 6.3 illustrates the aggregate picture. If certain restrictive assumptions are made (for example that there are no income effects and that aggregation across individuals is possible) the sum of surpluses from all consumers (for demand D_2 and admission charge A_2) would be represented by ABC in the figure. Johnson and Thomas (1989b) give an estimate of this aggregate consumers' surplus derived from Beamish by visitors. The estimate inevitably involved further assumptions – for example on the linearity of the demand curve – but it is probably the best available, given data limitations. Interestingly, the estimated consumer surplus more than covers the revenue subsidy provided by the local authorities. This consumers' surplus could of course be extracted by the Museum if perfect price discrimination were possible. Since such discrimination is not feasible, other techniques would have to be explored by the Museum if it were to attempt to convert the consumers' surplus into a financial flow. One possibility would be further promotion of other ways of giving to the Museum. Of course visitors may be reluctant to part with their surplus, especially given their perceived ability to free-ride (to enjoy the Museum's benefits while others pay for its provision).

Secondly, some demand for the Museum may not involve an

actual visit. For example, as Chapter 1 suggested, some individuals may value the Museum because it provides them with the *option* of visiting, even though they may never exercise that option. They may also wish to preserve the option for future generations or for others in the current generation. These options will not be maintained if the tasks of collection and preservation are not undertaken: as Atkinson recognized (see p.17), the opportunity to view buildings and other exhibits from the past may be lost for ever if appropriate action is not taken. The scale of option demand in respect of Beamish is not known, but it would be surprising if it did not exist in a significant way. Thirdly, even where option demand does not exist, there may remain a demand for the presence of the Museum, simply because it is regarded as 'a good thing' to have a repository for artefacts from the region's industrial and social history.

It may be very difficult to tap that demand for the Museum which is not expressed through the visitor demand curve. The desire to free-ride may be present and, in any case, it may be difficult to formulate suitable mechanisms for developing income from this demand. However, the US experience referred to earlier suggests that at the very least the issue might be explored further. A key question is whether US experience is specific to US culture.

6.3.3 Associated employment
The scope for Beamish to enhance employment in associated activities is limited. Planning restrictions in the immediate vicinity of the Museum impose severe limits on what can be done. As far as existing surrounding activities are concerned, the possibilities for further active promotion, through the provision of information and collaborative marketing, are not extensive. All these activities are small scale and the scope for further expansion is again limited by planning restrictions.

A more plausible option would be for the Museum itself to develop its own ancillary activities (hotels, restaurants, leisure facilities, shops) within the boundaries of the Museum. (These activities would not be 'associated' in the terminology of Chapter 4 since they would be inside the Museum). But such developments raise a number of questions. The first is the commercial viability of such operations. The highly seasonal nature of the visitor flows and the vulnerability of those flows to competition from elsewhere and to economic recession are likely to limit their attractiveness. Secondly, the development of ancillary activities may affect the nature of the Museum itself. It might be argued for example that extensive commercial activities detract from the underlying purpose of the Museum. Yet there may be ways, for example zoning of the Museum site, in which any adverse effect could be minimized. Finally, planning restrictions may also impose limitations on internal development.

6.3.4 Indirect employment

As Table 6.3, which is derived from the analysis of the Museum's invoices (Table A3.3) shows, the Museum derives 72 per cent of its purchases on its revenue account from inside the region. The corresponding percentage for capital expenditure is 77. Increased local sourcing would of course generate greater employment in the reference area. The elasticity of key activity indirect jobs with respect to the percentage of supplies locally serviced is about 1.57.[8] If the present level of the key activity's imports of supplies of materials into the reference area were to fall from the present 27 per.cent to 10 per cent then (assuming that this lower import propensity were reflected right down the chain of suppliers) indirect employment

Table 6.3   Location of Beamish suppliers

Category of expenditure	% of total expenditure in category		
	Inside North-East	Outside North-East	Total
Revenue expenditure	72	28	100
Capital expenditure	77	23	100
Total expenditure	73	27	100

Note: The figures in this table are derived from the data in Table A3.3 (p.112). Expenditure involving an 'unknown location' supplier is ignored. It should be noted that the 'location' of a supplier is not unambiguously defined. The Museum may well pay an invoice to an accounts or sales department of a company whose location is different from that of the production or distribution establishment. Even where this problem does not exist it must still be acknowledged that the location of suppliers to the Museum may not be a good guide to the location of the supply chain to those suppliers. In the above analysis, purchases were wholly allocated to the address to which the payment was made.

would rise from 41 jobs (see Table 4.1) to 57 jobs. These figures include only the increased indirect jobs and there would be consequent further induced jobs. How far it is possible to increase local sourcing beyond its current high proportion will depend, *inter alia*, on the present level and nature of the key activity's requirements, relative to the available supplies in the reference area, and on the extent to which local suppliers could be encouraged to set up and/or expand.

6.3.5   Induced employment
As the beginning of this chapter indicated, such employment is dependent on factors which largely lie outside the control of management and are not therefore considered here.

6.3.6   Diverted employment
The extent to which the Museum diverts employment from elsewhere in the region is determined by a range of complex and interacting factors. However it is likely that the more renowned the Museum becomes on a national level, the lower is the diversion within the reference area likely to be, since visitors will be attracted to the area who would not otherwise have come. The Museum is undoubtedly becoming more attractive to 'outsiders', as evidence from the Museum's own visitor surveys show. In 1981, 46 per cent of peak-period visitors came from outside the North-East; in 1989, this figure had risen to about 70 per cent.

6.4   Public policy
Public policy at both central and local government levels impinges in a variety of ways on the employment that arises from Beamish. The scale of public funding provided, the constraints placed on managers in relation to their pricing freedom, planning controls and general economic policy, are examples of the ways in which government may influence the different categories of employment identified in Figure 4.1. In this section, the discussion focuses on one key issue: the scale of public funding.

Table 6.4 provides some comparisons of the extent of public funding across the museums examined in Appendix 8. The two measures used in this table are the revenue subsidy per visitor and the relative importance of public funds as a source of income. In interpreting these figures, it must be remembered that most of the museums also receive subsidies in kind. Beamish and the Black

Table 6.4   Revenue subsidies

	Financial year ending (£)	Revenue subsidy per visitor (£)	Revenue subsidy as % of admission income *plus* revenue subsidy
Beamish	31.3.89	0.65	23
Black Country	31.3.89	0.42	17
Ironbridge	31.12.88	0.02	1
Ulster Folk and Transport	31.3.89	10.20	95
Welsh Folk	31.3.89	6.87	79
Arnhem	31.12.88	6.74	86
Zuiderzee	31.12.88	5.97	96
Skansen	31.12.88	1.51	65
Maihaugen	31.12.88	5.68	78
Norwegian Folk (Oslo)	31.12.88	6.86	86

Source: Appendix 8.

Country Museum receive administrative and accounting assistance from their respective local authorities which is not reflected in the figures. It is estimated that Ironbridge receives £150 000 in kind from Telford Development Corporation. This museum also has education staff seconded to it by the County Council (and Wreken District Council exempts the museum's buildings from rates). The Welsh Folk Museum benefits from services provided by the central management of the National Museum for Wales. The revenue subsidy in Table 6.4 is therefore the *non-earmarked cash* grant made by public sector funding agencies.

The relatively low average level of public revenue subsidy per visitor in the three non-national museums in the UK is immediately striking. (Ironbridge receives virtually no revenue support from the public sector.) The subsidy for each visitor to Beamish is less than one-fifteenth of that provided for the visitor to the Ulster Folk and Transport Museum. The subsidy to Beamish (and the Black Country Museum and Ironbridge) is also low by international standards.

In the last column of Table 6.4 the revenue subsidy is expressed as a percentage of the revenue subsidy *plus* admission income. (These two sources of income may be seen as income arising directly from the existence of the museums themselves rather than from ancillary activities such as catering and retailing.) Clearly, the revenue subsidy is much less important in these terms for the non-national museums, reflecting the relatively higher admission charges in the latter (Johnson and Thomas, 1990b).

Table 6.4 does not deal with capital expenditure. It has not been possible to collect detailed information on the financing of capital investment beyond the overall figure given in the table in Appendix 8. However, only Ironbridge relies to any extent on raising capital funds from the private sector.

It is very unlikely that Beamish will be able to increase its local authority funding – for either revenue or capital – beyond its present real level. Substantially increased funding from national sources would only come about if there were a change in the Museum's status or in government policy towards museums in the regions. Neither scenario is likely in the foreseeable future.

Although a significant increase in public funding for Beamish is not a realistic expectation – indeed a fall in such funding is more probable – it is nevertheless appropriate on the basis of the data given above to ask, first, is *any* public funding of Beamish justified; and, secondly, assuming the answer is yes, is the *relative* position of Beamish appropriate?

On the first question, it is not difficult to suggest reasons why a private market solution might generate a socially suboptimal allocation of resources to Beamish and why, therefore, there might be grounds for public assistance (for a review of the rationale for the public funding of museums, see Johnson and Thomas, 1991b). Some reasons why the private 'demand' for Beamish may be greater than that expressed in admission revenues have already been advanced elsewhere in this book. There may also be wider reasons. Society as a whole may place a higher valuation on (say) the ability of future generations to look at their past, than the aggregate of individuals' valuations. Again a positive value may be placed by society on the greater sense of regional identity generated by the Museum. Given the region's history of depression and unemployment this sense of identity takes on a particular importance.

As Chapter 4 argued, the presence of the Museum may also enhance the general quality of life in the region and hence increase the attractiveness of the region to (say) incoming industry. Another argument for public funding arises from the nature of research output. It may not be possible for the Museum to capture the returns from all of the research it undertakes (indeed if it were able to do so, the outcome would be socially suboptimal since the socially optimal charge for information already produced is zero).

Unfortunately there is no hard evidence on the precise scale of the benefits produced by the Museum which are not reflected in the visitor demand schedule. So it is not possible on present evidence to say whether the current level of public funding for Beamish is optimal.

As far as the relative position of Beamish is concerned, it is difficult to see an obvious rationale for the very substantial differences in the scale of public funding shown in Table 6.4. The national museums are of course much more strongly research orientated, but this in turn begs the question of why this should be so. It is almost certain that the marginal product of a unit of research resource in Beamish would be higher than that in the Welsh and Ulster Folk Museums simply because the scale of the current research effort is so much greater in the two national museums. There are strong political and historical reasons for the present allocation, yet it does not follow that social welfare is maximized by this allocation. Comparisons in public funding between the museum sector as a whole and other sectors are even more problematic than those between museums. However, in view of the focus of this study on employment, it is worth devoting a little attention to one particular measure of the returns from public expenditure in different uses: cost-per-job comparisons.

In many respects it is notoriously difficult to attach meaning to these comparisons – not least because they say nothing about job quality or duration – but they are made here because cost-per-job data have been widely used in policy discussions on the key issue of the efficiency of public expenditure for job creation. Myerscough (1988: 149) has argued that 'the arts were a cheaper way to create extra jobs than other forms of public revenue spending', and the Beamish figures do not seem out of line with his estimates, as Table 6.5 shows. The figures shown in this table exclude capital expenditure because Myerscough does not present data on this, but some idea of capital cost per job in tourism can be derived from data on the assistance to tourism projects payable under Section 4 of the Development of Tourism Act 1969. Counting direct jobs only, the

Table 6.5   Cost-per-job figures

Museums and galleries	Cost-per-job in terms of public revenue expenditure
in Glasgow	£1 363
in Merseyside	£2 658
in Ipswich	£1 778
Beamish Museum	£1 855

Sources: Myerscough (1988) and present study.

cost per job was £5 000. A comparable figure for Beamish might be in the order of £2 250.

The conclusion from these figures is that if job creation were the sole criterion for the allocation of public funds, and if the average figures quoted reflected marginal values, then transfer of such funds into the museum sector from elsewhere would be warranted. They also suggest that as far as capital expenditure in the tourism industry is concerned, expenditure on Beamish has a greater employment effect.

Conclusion

This chapter has examined some of the likely determinants of future employment generation at Beamish. It has also considered relevant policy issues. While employment creation is not a primary objective of either the Museum's management or the sponsoring local authorities, it will almost certainly result from increased income. It is doubtful whether significant real growth in income will now come from public sources. Rightly or wrongly, continued further expansion of the labour force at Beamish is likely to be heavily dependent on raising spending by visitors and the contribution of private individuals and institutions. As incomes rise generally, spending on leisure activities rises more than proportionately. How far Beamish benefits from that increased expenditure will depend on its competitive position, relative not only to other museums but also to other organizations offering outlets for leisure spending.

Notes
1.   Some of the discussion in this chapter draws on Johnson and Thomas (1991c, 1991d).

2. Figure 6.1 clearly shows that there are many fluctuations within the period but as a crude measure taking start and end points does not give a misleading picture.
3. It cannot be emphasized too strongly that this is a very crude categorization. Each museum differs from others in its products and presentation. The concern here is with identifying the differences that are crucial, but also recognizing that in labelling a museum as a particular type we are making a judgement about its general emphasis rather than an exact statement about all its characteristics.
4. Colonial Williamsburg is not directly comparable with Beamish, since it has restored buildings on their *original* sites. It is operated on an altogether more substantial basis and has benefited from large-scale endowment funding. However, it does provide an important illustration of the point made in the text. Other US museums much closer in purpose and scale to Beamish, for example Old Sturbridge Village in Sturbridge, Massachusetts, run their own hotel operations.
5. Only on very rare occasions has the Museum stopped further entry because of capacity constraints: provided visitors are prepared to queue they are admitted. However, it is plausible to suppose that the longer the queues at the turnstiles, the higher the turnround rate is likely to be.
6. Colonial Williamsburg, *1989 Annual Report*, p.21.
7. Plimoth Plantation Inc., *Financial Statements as of December 31, 1989 together with Auditor's Report*, p.3.
8. This rough estimate is based on the slope coefficient of a double log regression of key activity indirect employment (E_{II_K}) on alternative values of the propensity to import from outside the reference area (m) (ranging from 0.1 to 0.35 taking intervals of 0.05). The regression was

$$\ln E_{II_K} = 44.006 + 1.565 \ln(1-m)$$
$$(0.006) \quad (0.021)$$

Appendix 1 Derivation of the market share index (Figure 2.2)

This index is based on the percentage of visitors to all major attractions in Northumbria who visited Beamish. Data for visitors attending major attractions in Northumbria were collected from the English Tourist Board's *Regional Factsheets* for various years. 'Major' historic properties were defined as those with over 30 000 visitors in 1980. 'Major' museums and art galleries were defined as those with over 50 000 visitors in 1980. Where an attraction had more than one year's data missing it was excluded. For those attractions with one year's data missing, estimates for the missing values were made.

The attractions included in the exercise are Housesteads, Chesters, Vindolanda, Wallington Hall, Dunstanburgh Castle, Lindisfarne Castle, Warkworth Castle and Hermitage, Raby Castle, Durham Castle, Alnwick Castle, Lindisfarne Priory, Barnard Castle, Preston Hall, Bowes Museum and of course Beamish.

Although the above method is the best that can be done given the available data, the following should be noted. First, the basis for exclusion (inclusion) is rather arbitrary. Durham Cathedral, for example, is excluded. Secondly, new attractions developed during the period, notably the Metro Centre, are necessarily excluded. This is a particularly important omission because Beamish's market share is likely to be affected by the scale of new entry. Unfortunately the available data could not easily be adjusted to include new attractions. Finally and perhaps most fundamentally it should be noted that Beamish not only competes with other *attractions*, but with many kinds of leisure expenditure including holidays abroad, restaurant meals, books and so on.

Despite the limitations of the data, the graph is likely to provide a broadly accurate indication of trends in Beamish's market share. (The removal of Preston Hall – the attraction with the largest recorded number of visitors – from the data makes no difference to these trends.)

Appendix 2 The relationship between employment and visitors, and between employment and admission revenue

Table A2.1   *Regression results using annual data for the financial years ending 1978 to 1989*

Dependent variable	Constant	Visitors (thousands)	R^2
Weekly staff	−26.18	0.249 (0.041)	0.78
Monthly staff	15.19	0.046 (0.015)	0.50
Total staff	−10.99	0.295 (0.051)	0.77

Dependent variable	Constant	Admission revenue £'000	R^2
Weekly staff	7.83	0.084 (0.005)	0.96
Monthly staff	21.14	0.016 (0.004)	0.68
Total staff	28.97	0.100 (0.006)	0.96

Appendix 3 The calculation of employment estimates

This Appendix uses the general framework outlined in Section 4.2 to estimate the gross and net employment impact of Beamish.

A3.1 Gross employment

A3.1.1 Direct employment in the key activity (the Museum)

This is the first term in equation (4.1) in Section 4.2. The employment estimate was based on the Museum's employment records and there was no need to calculate S and e separately. The employment figures are the average for the whole year (in terms of full-time equivalents). Thus the problem of seasonal activity is accommodated. Table A3.1 presents the results of the calculations.

Table A3.1   Direct employment in the key activity (Beamish)

		Feb.[1]	Aug.[1]	Average
Monthly Staff	Full-time	47	43	
	Part-time	0	0	
Weekly staff	Full-time	53	124	
	Part-time	20	19	
Total employed by the Museum (Full-time equivalents)[2]		110	186.5	148.25
Franchise staff[3]				7.5
				155.75

1. Figures refer to the first complete week in the relevant month.
2. Part-time counted as half.
3. These were employed in the Sun Inn, the stables, the photographer's, and ice-cream sales.

A3.1.2 Direct employment in associated activity

This is the second term in equation (4.2) in Section 4.2. Employment in associated activity is

108

[Total expenditure in the North-East outside Beamish]
× [Attribution factor]
÷ [Sales–employment ratio]

The total expenditure in the North-East, outside the Museum, was estimated from a sample survey of visitors undertaken in the summer of 1989 (see Appendix 5), as £11 839 651. This figure was based on the visitor expenditure data obtained from the survey, grossed up to obtain a spending figure for all visitors. This grossing up can be done by multiplying the survey expenditure data by the ratio either of the total number of visitors to the number of visitors in the survey, or of the total visitor spending inside Beamish (obtainable from the Museum's accounts) to the spending inside Beamish of the visitors in the sample survey. The latter assumes that the same relationship also holds for spending outside Beamish. In the present calculations the average of the two methods was taken.

In order to assess whether this expenditure was attributable to the Museum, visitors in the survey were asked further questions to ascertain whether their spending in the region was dependent on the existence of Beamish. If it was dependent on Beamish then the expenditure can be said to be attributable to Beamish. Figure A3.1 shows the questions put to Museum visitors who were staying in the region and the way the answers could be used to assess attribution. A similar procedure was followed with day trippers, as shown in Figure A3.2.

On the basis of these questions it was possible to establish the attribution factor for each category of visitor and to calculate an overall attribution factor as a weighted average of these. For expenditure outside Beamish the overall attribution factor was about 8.5 per cent, as Table A3.2 shows.

The attributable expenditure was divided by a sales–employment ratio to estimate the associated employment. The sales–employment ratio used is the unweighted average of the sales–employment ratios of sectors which are likely to be the principal destinations of visitors' spending flows outside Beamish, that is, retailing, hotels, transport and other services. The 1989 figure was £32 134. This includes VAT.

The associated direct employment is thus

$$(\pounds 11\ 839\ 651 \times 0.0848) \div \pounds 32\ 134 = 31.2 \text{ jobs}$$

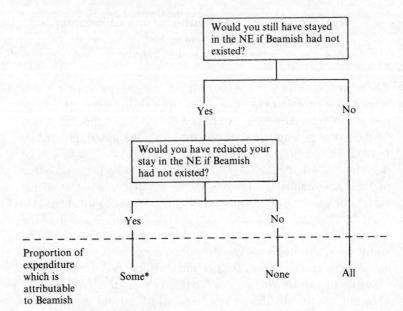

* In the case of respondents who answered yes to both questions a further question
  was put: 'By how many nights would you have reduced your stay?' The answer to
  this, as a proportion of the total nights stayed, could then be used as an estimate of
  the proportion of expenditure attributable.

*Figure A3.1   Attribution questions for Museum visitors staying in the
North-East*

A3.1.3   Indirect employment stemming from the key activity

This is the first term in equation (4.2). The first-round effects were
calculated separately. These were based on a detailed examination of
the Museum's purchases of supplies. A complete analysis of all
invoices, covering both revenue and capital expenditure, enabled all
the purchases in the North-East to be identified and classified by
product group. This was a very detailed exercise. Data, from the
Census of Production, input–output tables and other sources were
used to calculate national employment–sales ratios for each category. These ratios were then applied to the figures of spending in
each category to derive the total first-round direct employment. (The
application of *national* ratios to the North-East has obvious limitations, but the data necessary to calculate regional figures are
unavailable.) Table A3.3 shows the results of this exercise.

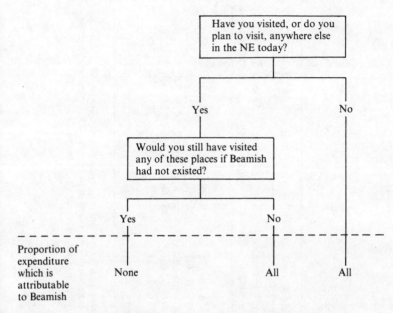

*Figure A3.2   Attribution questions for Museum visitors who are day
trippers*

Table A3.2   The attribution factor

Category of visitor[1]	Attribution factor
Local home-based day trippers	0.6795
Non-local home-based day trippers	1.0000
Other day trippers	0.9772
Stayers	0.0482
Total	0.0848

1. See Section 5.2 for a brief description of each category.

The calculation of subsequent rounds of indirect employment was
found by applying a multiplier formula to capture the backward
linkages in the chain of suppliers. The multiplier was based on the
following estimates:

Table A3.3 First-round indirect employment effects, 1987–8[1]

Category of expenditure	Inside North-East		Outside North-East		Unknown location		Total	
	Sales £	Estimated employment	Sales £	Estimated employment	Sales £	Estimated employment	Sales £	Estimated employment
Revenue expenditure								
Shop expenditure	102 137	(2)	113 376	(2)	9 188	(–)	224 701	(4)
Non-shop expenditure	378 653	(8)	116 315	(4)	36 980	(1)	531 948	(13)
Local authorities	98 970	(5)	not applicable		not applicable		98 970	(5)
Total, revenue expenditure	579 760	(15)	229 691	(6)	46 168	(1)	856 618	(22)
Capital expenditure	187 372	(7)	56 331	(2)	9 375	(–)	253 078	(9)
Total, revenue and capital expenditure	767 132	(22)	286 022	(8)	55 543	(1)	1 108 696	(31)

1. Figures in brackets are based on, or include, employment estimates derived from the relevant employment–sales ratios for the North-East. Thus, for example, estimated employment from shop expenditure outside the North-East is derived by applying the employment–sales ratio for shop expenditure in the North-East (2/£102 137) to the sales figure for shop expenditure outside the North-East (£113 376).

$$p = 0.47$$
$$m_f = 0.27$$

p   the proportion of sales revenue which is spent on supplies, was approximated by total intermediate expenditure on goods and services (less taxes and expenditure plus subsidies) as a proportion of total input. The national figure (calculated from the *Input-Output Tables for the United Kingdom, 1984*, London: HMSO, 1988, Table 4) was used as the best available estimate.

m_f the marginal propensity of firms to import supplies into the North-East, was assumed to be the same as the Beamish first-round figure of imports into the region.

c   the employment–sales ratio, was assumed to be the same throughout the chain of suppliers. The first-round ratio derived directly from the Beamish data was (implicitly) used throughout, i.e. the multiplier calculated on the basis of the values of p and m_f was simply applied to the number of jobs, 22, in the first-round.

The multiplier was $[1 - 0.47(1 - 0.27)]^{-1} = 1.5223$ which gave total indirect jobs as 33.49 jobs. This figure is for 1988 and has been increased by the rate of growth of jobs in Beamish during 1988–9 to provide an estimate of 1989 jobs, i.e. $33.49 \times 1.223 = 40.96$ jobs.

A3.1.4   Indirect employment stemming from the associated activities

This is the second term in equation (4.2). The total (attributable) expenditure on associated activity was £11 939 651 × 0.0848 = £1 004 002. Using the same values for p and m_f as in the Beamish indirect calculations (see above) gives first-round spending on supplies of $S_p(1 - m_f)$, i.e.

$$£1\ 004\ 002 \times 0.47 \times (1 - 0.27) = £344\ 473$$

To find the number of jobs that this represents, this figure is divided by the appropriate sales–employment ratio. The figure used here was that for food, drink and tobacco wholesaling, i.e. £150 788, as much of the expenditure on supplies was in this sector. First-round indirect employment is thus 344 473/150 788 = 2.28 jobs, which, when using the same multiplier for the backward linkages as in the Beamish indirect case (1.52) gives a total of 2.37 jobs.

A3.1.5   Induced employment

The induced employment has been calculated directly by taking the sum of direct and indirect employment and applying a multiplier to this. The multiplier is a Keynesian income multiplier and it is assumed that this exactly matches the process of employment generation. The parameter values used are

$$c = 0.909$$
$$t = 0.209$$
$$m_c = 0.872$$

c   is derived from *Regional Trends 24, 1989 Edition*, London: HMSO, 1989, Tables 12.6 and 12.7, p. 139. It is the ratio of consumers' expenditure in the North to personal disposable income in the Northern Standard Region.

t   is derived from the same source as c and is the ratio of the difference between total personal income and personal disposable income, to total personal income.

  Both c and t are derived from data which relate to the whole of the Northern Standard Region, rather than just the North-East, and are for 1986. These data are the best and latest available.

m_c is taken as the ratio of imports to the Northern region to GDP at market prices in the Northern region. The source is Northern Region Strategy Team (1976), Table 27. Although the figures are for 1971 they are the best available. There are no grounds for believing that the net changes in the Northern economy over the last two decades would lead to a change in this figure one way or the other.

  The value of the multiplier for calculating induced employment is thus

$$[1 - (0.909 \times 0.791 \times 0.128)]^{-1} = 1.101$$

This of course includes the base employment (the direct plus indirect) so the induced employment is 0.101 × (direct + indirect employment). This is shown in Table A3.4.

Table A3.4   Induced employment

Activity	Beamish	Associated
Direct + indirect employment	197	35
Induced employment[1]	20	4

1. Rounded to the nearest integer.

A3.2 Net employment

Estimates of diverted employment are based on estimates of diverted expenditure derived from the visitor survey. Visitors were asked what they would have done with their money if Beamish had not existed. They were offered alternatives as follows:

Would have spent it on other tourist/leisure activities in the North-East;
Would have spent it on other tourist/leisure activities outside the North-East;
Would have increased general spending a bit;
Would have saved a bit more;
Other;
Not sure.

It may reasonably be supposed that *all* the expenditure which would have been on other 'tourist/leisure activities in the North-East' is diverted. This, by itself, would therefore provide a minimum estimate of diverted expenditure. It may be that some or all of 'general spending' might represent diverted expenditure. If all of this were assumed to be diverted, and the amount were added to that diverted from tourist/leisure activities in the North-East, then it may be supposed that this is a maximum estimate of diverted expenditure.

Before proceeding further it is appropriate to acknowledge some limitations surrounding the estimation of diverted expenditure by this kind of questionnaire response. Answers to questions in which respondents are asked to describe behaviour in hypothetical situations must be treated cautiously for there is no way of knowing whether a particular casual 'thought experiment' is a good guide to what people would actually do if faced with a real situation. Furthermore there may be some bias in the estimates arising from the fact that respondents were limited to one response. Thus only one alternative use of money could be identified. It would have been impractical to seek more sophisticated information but the principal source of the spending on Beamish is likely to have been identified. There is reason for some confidence in the results. The question was in fact well answered: only 3 per cent of respondents answered 'not sure' and the variations and similarities in response across visitor categories were plausible. In any case, there does not seem to be a better way of estimating diverted expenditure.

The minimum and maximum diversion factors estimated from the survey were 71.1 per cent and 80.9 per cent, i.e. 76 per cent on average.

Having established the diversion factor on the basis of expenditure a crucial step follows. The diverted *expenditure* needs to be converted into *employment* terms. If it is assumed, reasonably in the face of data limitations, that the marginal employment–sales ratio relating to the gross employment (i.e. the increment in gross employment divided by the increment in total expenditure giving rise to this employment) is equal to the marginal employment–sales ratio relating to diverted expenditure (i.e. the increment in diverted employment divided by the increment in diverted expenditure) then it can be shown that the diversion factor based on *expenditure*, may be used to calculate net employment from gross *employment*.

Let N = net employment
$\quad\;\; G$ = gross employment
$\quad\;\; D$ = diverted employment
$\quad\;\; GX$ = gross expenditure
$\quad\;\; DX$ = diverted expenditure
$\quad\;\; d$ = the proportion of expenditure diverted
$\quad\;\; e_{GX}$ = the marginal employment–sales ratio for total expenditure giving rise to gross employment
$\quad\;\; e_{DX}$ = the marginal employment–sales ratio for diverted expenditure

Definitionally

$$N = G - D$$
$$G = (GX)e_{GX}$$
$$D = (DX)e_{DX}$$
$$(DX) = d(GX)$$

Therefore

$$N = (GX)e_{GX} - d(GX)e_{DX}$$

Now if $e_{GX} = e_{DX}$, then

$$N = (1 - d)G$$

In practice average employment–sales ratios are used as an approximation for the marginal ratios.

The total gross employment, shown in Table 4.1, is 256 so the diverted employment, $D = dG$, is 195 jobs, and the net employment, $N = (1 - d)G$, is 61 jobs.

It has been assumed throughout that $\lambda = 1$ because there is a sufficient slack in the North-East labour market for there to be no difficulty in recruiting.

Appendix 4 A note on the size of the reference area

The proposition that the size of the reference area is of crucial importance in interpreting the calculated net employment can be illustrated by a simple example which is presented in Figure A4.1. The figure is based on a number of assumptions.

(i) The size of the reference area is shown on the horizontal axis. Areas are arbitrarily designated by letters. The area labelled 'size A' might be thought to represent an area identical to the boundaries of the Museum (so there is zero additional employment and by assumption zero diverted employment). 'Size B' might be an area, say 5 miles' radius around the Museum, 'size C' a slightly bigger area, and so on until the largest area ('size Q') which might be thought of as the economy as a whole.

(ii) At the level of the whole economy it is assumed in this particular example that there is total diversion, that is all the gains in employment are completely offset by displaced employment so that the net employment impact is zero. This assumption is of course one extreme view (though one which often figures in policy discussions of zero-sum games). In practice displaced employment may be small if there is expenditure diversion from abroad, or if there is a growing economy, or if there are unemployed resources.

(iii) The figure is drawn on the basis of hypothetical data presented in Table A4.1. The area labelled 'size E' approximates the 'North-East' in our study of Beamish. It shows a Museum with direct employment of 160, generating additional employment of 100, so gross employment is 260. The diversion factor is 0.75 which means that 195 jobs are displaced elsewhere in the region leaving net employment of 65. These employment levels are similar to those shown in Table 4.2.

This picture of our reference area is entirely consistent with very different net employment impacts for smaller- and larger-sized reference areas, as shown in Figure A4.1. It is clear, given the assumptions made, that net employment *must* vary with the size of the reference area and this should be acknowledged in any discussion of

Table A4.1 Data for Figure A4.1: numbers employed

Size	Museum direct employment	Additional employment	Gross employment G	Diversion factor d	Diverted employment dG	Net employment $(1-d)G$
A	160	0	160	0.00	0	160
B	160	30	190	0.30	57	133
C	160	60	220	0.50	110	110
D	160	80	240	0.65	156	84
E	160	100	260	0.75	195	65
F	160	120	280	0.80	224	56
G	160	135	295	0.82	242	53
H	160	150	310	0.84	260	50
J	160	165	325	0.86	280	46
K	160	180	340	0.88	299	41
L	160	190	350	0.90	315	35
M	160	195	355	0.92	327	28
N	160	200	360	0.95	342	18
P	160	200	360	0.98	353	7
Q	160	200	360	1.00	360	0

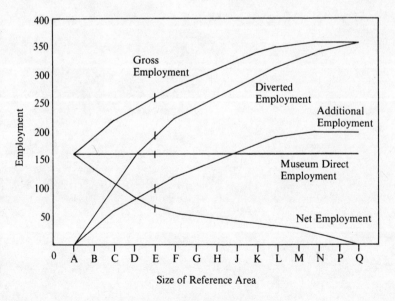

Figure A4.1 Employment by size of reference area

employment impact. If, for example, some smaller reference area had been taken, say size B, then there would almost certainly be less additional, but much less diverted employment, giving higher net employment of 133 in this example. And similarly a larger reference area than E would yield smaller net employment.

It is a simple matter to vary the assumptions and compute alternative scenarios, though this is not done here as the purpose is simply to demonstrate that the size of the reference area is relevant for estimating net impact.

Appendix 5   The visitor survey at Beamish

The results in Chapter 4 and the discussion in the first part of Chapter 5 draw on the results of a visitor survey conducted by the authors in August 1989 (see Johnson and Thomas, 1990a). This Appendix discusses key characteristics of the survey.

A5.1   The conduct of the survey

The survey was carried out over 14 consecutive days between Monday 31 July and Sunday 13 August 1989. As Table A5.1 shows, this was a peak period for visitor flows. However as indicated by Table A5.2, there were considerable daily variations in visitor numbers

Table A5.1   Monthly visitor totals, 1989

January	3 818	July	78 359
February	8 145	August	111 315
March	36 594	September	49 645
April	26 487	October	33 289
May	56 519	November	9 229
June	69 794	December	3 371

with the peak day in the fortnight (Sunday 13 August; 4 954 visitors) being more than twice as high as that for the lowest day (Friday 11 August; 2 223 visitors). The weather during this period was particularly good even for August. Only two days (Wednesday 9 August and Friday 11 August) experienced prolonged rain.

For most of the questions the sampling unit was *the individual*, although expenditure data related to *the immediate party* of which the individual was a member. Only adults (defined as those aged over 16) were approached.

The survey was conducted outside the main entrance of the Museum by two trained interviewers. Interviews were conducted between 1.00 p.m. and 4.30 p.m. each day. Very few visitors leave the Museum before 1.00 p.m. (the Museum opens at 10.00 a.m.). The

Table A5.2   Total visitors, 31 July–13 August 1989

	Total visitors	Interviews
31 July (Mon.)	3 332	39
1 August (Tues.)	4 285	41
2 August (Wed.)	4 884	40
3 August (Thur.)	4 043	40
4 August (Fri.)	2 875	40
5 August (Sat.)	2 545	40
6 August (Sun.)	4 050	40
7 August (Mon.)	3 470	40
8 August (Tues.)	4 734	40
9 August (Wed.)	2 810	40
10 August (Thur.)	3 176	40
11 August (Fri.)	2 223	42
12 August (Sat.)	2 383	38
13 August (Sun.)	4 954	40
TOTAL	49 764	560

decision to stop interviewing at 4.30 p.m. reflected the management's desire for the substantial numbers of visitors leaving after that time not to be impeded at the exit. This restriction inevitably gives rise to the possibility of bias (see below). Individuals were approached as they left the Museum. The selection of the adult interviewees within the interview period was undertaken on a random basis.

Interviewees were told at the outset of the interview that the survey was an independent one and part of a larger study being undertaken by the University of Durham into the economic impact of Beamish. The full questionnaire was piloted in early May 1989, using a sample of 20 respondents. Some small modifications were made to the questionnaire as a result of the pilot. The full questionnaire is reproduced in Johnson and Thomas (1990a). Some of the questions were taken straight from the Museum's own exit survey – which was suspended during the interview period – at the request of the Museum's management. For some of the questions interviewees were provided with a card giving alternative answers from which to choose. Interviews lasted about 10 minutes. The majority of questions were pre-coded.

In all, 560 adults were interviewed, representing 1.4 per cent of the

39 428 adults visiting the Museum during the period. Interviews were spread evenly throughout the 14-day period (Table A5.2). The numbers of adults and children in the parties represented by these 560 adults are given in Table 5.3. In total 2.8 per cent of adults and 3.9 per cent of children were 'represented' through the interviews.

The non-response rate was low: 5.6 per cent of 593 adults approached refused to co-operate. The reasons given were as follows.

	Number of refusals
Transport waiting	11
Other reasons	10
Reason(s) not specified	12
	33

The biggest single reason was the imminent departure of public or private transport. ('Other reasons' included deafness, 'dog in car', 'tired', 'too wet'). It is unlikely that non-response is a significant source of bias in the results.

A5.2   Possible sources of bias
The most likely sources of bias in the survey were as follows.

A5.2.1   The period chosen
It is possible that peak-period visitors may differ in their characteristics from off-peak visitors. The former may be more likely to come from outside the region and to be on a more extended holiday trip. They may also be more likely to bring children. The fact that interviewees go to the Museum when it is very busy and its facilities more fully utilized may also influence what they do when in the Museum and their perceptions of it. However, an off-peak survey conducted by the authors as a check on the main survey did not indicate that the results of the latter were unrepresentative in any significant way relevant to this study.

A5.2.2   The sampling unit
There may be a source of bias arising from the fact that the respondent was speaking on behalf of the party as a whole. For simple factual information such as the duration of the visit this is unlikely to be a problem as the behaviour of all members of the party is likely

to be accurately described by the respondent. But where individual perceptions are concerned (for example the possibility of returning, or value for money), the respondent might not accurately describe the views of all members of the party.

A closely related point is that each member of the party may not be in the same category as the respondent. A common example would be where local residents have some visitors from outside the North-East staying with them and decide to take them to Beamish for the afternoon. Information on the extent to which parties were 'mixed' in this sense is not available, and we have treated all members as if they were in the same class as the respondent.

A5.2.3 The weather

A visitor's activities in, and perceptions of, an open-air museum such as Beamish are inevitably affected by weather conditions. Whereas (for example) a shortage of cover is largely irrelevant on a sunny day, it becomes very significant when there is heavy rain. As indicated earlier, the interview period was a particularly fine spell. This must be borne in mind in any interpretation of the data.

A5.2.4 The timing of the interview

The start and finish times of the afternoon interview period may have excluded a particular type of visitor. For example, disgruntled visitors who arrived when the Museum opened may have left before 1.00 p.m. Conversely, those leaving after 4.30 p.m. may have found the Museum particularly good value for money, hence their willingness to stay later. No tests which would gauge the extent of such bias were possible.

A5.2.5 Response bias

It is possible that some interviewees responded to questions in a way designed to impress or influence the interviewer and/or the Museum management. It is likely however that such bias was minimal given that interviewers stressed the independent and confidential nature of the survey. Furthermore, inaccuracies in responses attributable to faulty recall are likely to be minimal since the interviews were conducted immediately following the visit.

A5.2.6 Daily variations

The number of interviews carried out each day was virtually constant throughout the survey period, though there were variations in the number of visitors as Table A5.2 has shown. If the characteristics of visitors differ on different days there may be some under/over-representation of particular types of visitor.

Appendix 6   The main categories of respondent

The following figure illustrates the questions that were put to visitors during the survey and which were used as a basis for categorizing visitors. The numbers in each category are shown. Note that the stayers category could be divided into local (i.e. those staying in the North-East and whose home was in the North-East) and non-local (those whose home was outside the North-East) but there were only 2 in the former group so both groups have been put together.

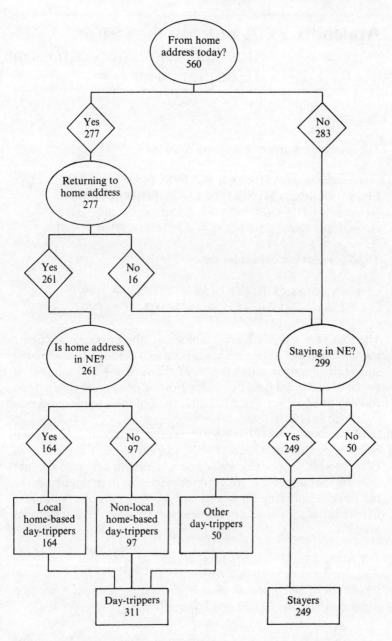

Figure A6.1   Categories of respondent

Appendix 7   A note on the visitor demand regression equation (Chapter 5)

The following diagnostic tests are reported:

Serial correlation: CHI-SQ(4) = 7.2690; F(4,36) = 1.4000
Functional form: CHI-SQ(1) = 1.6640; F(1,39) = 1.2400
Normality: CHI/SQ(2) = 0.9387; F statistic not applicable
Heteroscedasticity: CHI-SQ(1) = 2.5583; F(1,52) = 2.5861

The 5 per cent critical values are as follows:

CHI-SQ(1): 3.84;   CHI-SQ(2): 5.99;   CHI-SQ(4): 9.49
F(4,36): 2.86;   F(1,39): 4.09;   F(1,52): 4.03

The four tests examined are, respectively, the Lagrange multiplier test of residual serial correlation, Ramsey's RESET test using the square of the fitted values, a test of the skewness and kurtosis of residuals and a test based on the regression of squared residuals on squared fitted values. For a full discussion of these tests see Pesaran and Pesaran (1987).

This equation was also subjected to a test of stability, estimating it over the period 1975Q1 to 1987Q1 and examining the predictions over the next six quarters with respect to the known outcomes; not only are the estimated coefficients little different from those from the full sample, but using Chow's second test for predictive failure, the hypothesis of stability cannot be rejected: the observed test statistics are:

CHI-SQ(6) = 8.0188;   F(6,34) = 1.3365

which are to be compared with critical values (using a 5 per cent significance level) of 12.59 and 2.38 respectively.

Appendix 8   Beamish: some international comparisons

To place the study of Beamish in a wider context, it was decided to examine some key open-air museums in the UK, and a small selection of similar museums abroad. In the UK, the Black Country Museum at Dudley, the Ironbridge Gorge Museum at Telford, the Ulster Folk and Transport Museum at Cultra, outside Belfast, and the Welsh Folk Museum near Cardiff were selected. On most criteria these would all be regarded as major open-air museums. There are numerous open-air museums overseas. After consultation with a number of experts in this field, it was decided to focus attention on three major museums in Scandinavia and two in the Netherlands. The three in Scandinavia were Skansen in Stockholm, Maihaugen in Lillehammer and the Norwegian Folk Museum near Oslo. Scandinavia was chosen because it is the 'home' of open-air museums: it is generally agreed that Skansen in Stockholm was the world's first open-air museum: the formation of many open-air museums including some of those studied here derived an important stimulus from the example of Skansen. It was also felt that the rural tradition of the Scandinavian museums would provide a useful focus for contrast with Beamish.

The museums in the Netherlands – the Netherlands Open Air Museum at Arnhem and the Zuiderzee museum at Enkhuizen – were selected because they also offered an interesting comparative perspective on the Beamish study. Arnhem, which is largely in the rural tradition, has been established for many years and has recently had to adapt to avoid closure. (It is currently being privatized.) The Zuiderzee museum on the other hand is a relative newcomer (despite a long 'gestation' period) see Johnson and Thomas (1990b) and its open-air displays are much less rural in character. All the museums selected for comparison also had to meet the criteria that a visit was possible within the research budget. They do of course represent only a very small proportion of the total: well over 150 open-air museums exist (Owen, 1988: 76). However, they are, by most standards, major open-air museums.

Table A8.1   Open-air museums: some comparative data for 1988–9

Museum	Date of opening	Organization	Objective
1. UNITED KINGDOM			
(i) Beamish, County Durham	1972[1]	Local authority consortium and managed by a joint committee	To study, collect, preserve and exhibit buildings, machinery, objects and information illustrating the historical development of industry and the way of life of the North of England ... to endeavour to deal comprehensively with the social, industrial and agricultural history of the region and to bring together the buildings and artefacts of recent centuries[2]
(ii) Black Country Museum, Dudley	1979	Trust, with some local authority representation	To secure for the benefit of the public the preservation, restoration, improvement, enhancement and maintenance of features and objects of historical and industrial interest in the Black Country area[5]
(iii) Ironbridge,[9] Telford	1973[10]	Trust, with some local authority representation	To secure the preservation, restoration, improvement, enhancement and maintenance of features and objects of historical and industrial interest in the area of Dawley New Town and the surrounding district of East Shropshire[11]
(iv) Ulster Folk and Transport Museum, Cultra	1964	National Museum with Board of Trustees	To illustrate the way of life past and present, and the traditions of the people of Northern Ireland[14]
(v) Welsh Folk Museum, Cardiff	1948	Part of a National Museum governed by a council which answers to the National Museum's Court of Governors	To illustrate the character and personality of the people of Wales from the point of view of human activity and to interpret them to the widest possible audience[20]

Period covered in open-air displays	Acreage	Total number of visitors	Employment	Admission income (£000s)	Public sector revenue grant (£000s)	Capital expenditure (£000s)
Immediately prior to First World War[3]	300	496 914	137[4]	1 100	321	302
1800 onwards	26	294 578	84[6]	612	124[7]	1 056[8]
Industrial Revolution onwards	n/a	404 226	180[12]	1 009	7[13]	476
Generation immediately prior First World War[15]	176[16]	161 474[17]	177[17,18]	420[17]	1 647[17,19]	501[17]
Not specified	98	288 593	156[21]	512	1 984	54

Table A8.1   continued

Museum	Date of opening	Organization	Objective
2. OVERSEAS: NETHERLANDS			
(i) Arnhem, OAM, Netherlands	1918	National Museum, governed by the Ministry of Culture	To present changes in the pattern of life in the Netherlands[20]
(ii) Zuiderzee Museum, Enkhuizen, Netherlands	1983	As above	To illustrate daily life and work around the Zuiderzee[20]
3. OVERSEAS: SCANDINAVIA			
(i) Skansen, Stockholm, Sweden	1891[28]	Independent foundation with major representation from central and regional government. Nordic Museum also represented	To show how people in the whole of Sweden but especially in rural areas, lived and the interaction between culture and nature (flora and fauna); and to have a continuous programme of events demonstrating various aspects of Swedish life[20]
(ii) Maihaugen Lillehammer, Norway	1904[31]	Independent foundation with representation from central, regional and local government. Friends also represented.	Based primarily on material culture, the museum shall constitute a 'memory' of society, creating understanding of historical connections and continuity and promoting tolerance and respect for cultural diversity[20]
(iii) Norwegian Folk Museum, Oslo, Norway	1901[36]	Independent foundation with representation from central and local Government	To show how the people of Norway from town and country, rich and poor have lived and worked[20]

Notes
1. A preliminary exhibition had been opened the previous year.
2. The Museum's first *Development Plan*, submitted to the Joint Committee of Local Authorities, 11 December 1970.
3. The collections policy of the museum is not so constrained.
4. The average of August 1988 and February 1989. A part-time employee is counted as 0.5.
5. Memorandum of Association of the Black Country Museum Trust Ltd, para. 3(A)

Period covered in open-air displays	Acreage	Total number of visitors	Employment	Admission income (£000s)	Public sector revenue grant (£000s)	Capital expenditure (£000s)
1600 onwards	108	370 939	121[22]	415[23]	2 500[23,24]	n/a[25]
Late 19th and early 20th century	30	290 000[26]	117[27]	270[23]	1 732[23,24]	n/a[25]
14th century to present day	75	1 685 474	190[29]	1 390[30]	2 550[30]	151[30]
From the 16th century to the present with special emphasis on the 20th century	90	139 000[32]	55[33]	226[34]	790[34]	zero[35]
From the 16th century to the present day	35	207 804	93[37]	226[34]	1 426[34,38]	2 230[34,39]

6. Made up of 79.5 'year-round' staff and 4 'year-round' full-time equivalents. The latter reflects the employment of seasonal staff.
7. Made up £122 900 general plant, plus an earmarked grant of £870.
8. This figure, which includes £846 206 from Dudley Metropolitan Borough Council for the development of a mine, was exceptional. In 1987–8, the capital investment figure was £306 000.
9. Ironbridge has seven major sites. Unless otherwise stated the data in this row apply to the whole of the Ironbridge complex.

10. This date refers to the opening of Blists Hill, the open-air section of Ironbridge.
11. Memorandum of Association of Ironbridge Gorge Trust Ltd, para. 3(A).
12. The average number of employees quoted in the annual report and accounts for both the Museum Trust and the Trading Company.
13. The amount provided in cash by the local authority. The latter also provides assistance in kind. Grants from all sources including companies amounted to £63 300 in 1988.
14. Ulster Folk Museum Act (Northern Ireland) 1958, Section 1.
15. The exhibitions mounted in the museum's galleries cover a longer period. The transport collection is not focused on a particular period.
16. Includes 40 acres for the Transport Museum.
17. Communication from the Director. The figure includes both Witham St and the Transport collection.
18. Average for the year 1988–9.
19. From the Northern Ireland Department of Education. The figure excludes transfers to capital accounts (£103 000).
20. This statement of objective was provided by the Director of the Museum in discussion with the authors.
21. Counts a part-time 'year-round' employee as 0.5, a full-time seasonal employee as 0.5, and a part-time seasonal employee as 0.25.
22. Average for the year; excludes franchise activities.
23. The exchange rate used is the average for 1988, £1 = DF1. 3.52 (*Financial Statistics 1989*, HMSO, July 1989, Table 13.2).
24. The gross payment made by the Ministry of Culture.
25. Capital expenditure is not separated out from revenue expenditure. All capital finance comes from the Ministry of Culture.
26. Includes 40 000 visitors to the indoor museum.
27. The average of peak and off-peak full-time equivalents.
28. This date refers to the opening of the present site at Skansen, on the outskirts of Stockholm. The founder of the museum had previously opened a small exhibition in Stockholm itself.
29. Average of peak and off-peak figures.
30. The exchange rate used is the average for 1988, £1 = SKR 10.90 (*Financial Statistics 1989*, HMSO, July 1989, Table 13.2).
31. A collection had been started in 1887.
32. Includes an estimated 25 000 'free' visitors.
33. Average for the year.
34. The exchange rate used is the average for 1988, £1 = NKR 11.52 (*Financial Statistics 1989*, HMSO, July 1989, Table 13.2).
35. Capital expenditure fluctuates considerably from year to year. For example in 1986 NKR 7 million was spent on a warehouse for the collections.
36. Relates to the opening of the present site. It grew out of a collection started by Hans Aall in 1894.
37. The average of the peak and off-peak figures.
38. Excludes grants for specific purposes (e.g. new exhibitions).
39. Capital expenditure fluctuates from year to year.

Each museum selected for the comparisons was visited (at least once), and its senior management interviewed. Information obtained from these interviews was supplemented with that obtained from museum records and relevant publications, such as de Jong (1988), Evans (1988), Hudson (1987), Longford (1972), Peate (1971) and Valen-Sendstad (1986).

Table A8.1 gives some indication of the key characteristics of the museums chosen for the comparisons. (In the case of Beamish, the Black Country Museum, the Ulster Folk and Transport Museum and the Welsh Folk Museum, the statistical data relate to the financial year ending March 1989. For the other museums the period covered is the calendar year 1988.) The table should be treated cautiously: as the notes to the table make clear, accurate comparable information on even basic characteristics is extremely difficult to obtain. In some cases the organization to which the information relates extends beyond the open-air museum. For example, the data on the Zuiderzee Museum includes the indoor museum. Many of the other museums also have extensive indoor collections. In one case, the Welsh Folk Museum, a castle forms part of the site. Skansen has its own zoo. The Ulster Folk and Transport Museum includes a transport collection on a separate site. Ironbridge covers seven major sites, only one of which, Blists Hill, is a conventional open-air museum. Ironbridge also runs, in conjunction with the University of Birmingham, the Ironbridge Institute, an organization designed for postgraduate training in industrial archaeology and heritage management. A further complication over the comparisons arises because the museums vary in the extent to which their retailing and catering activities are franchised. However, wherever possible franchised operations are included in the data in Table A8.1.

Difficulties over definitions of financial and other variables also exist. For example, what is regarded as 'capital investment' in one museum, may sometimes be included under revenue account 'maintenance' in another. Again the measurement of 'employment' is not straightforward where seasonal and/or part-time staff are involved. Even the counting of visitor numbers raises difficulties. At Ironbridge for example, visitors can pay for individual attractions or they can purchase a 'passport' ticket from any site, which covers admission to all sites. (The Ironbridge data used in this paper refer to *the numbers of individuals who purchased tickets*. The number of *site visits* is considerably higher: more than double ticket purchases.)

Furthermore, the use of official exchange rates in the data for the overseas museums is not entirely satisfactory. However, even allowing for these difficulties, it is apparent from the table that a variety of organizational forms and objectives are covered. The museums' scale and financial arrangements also vary. Furthermore, while some museums, notably those in Scandinavia, have their origins in the last century, others are post-Second World War developments.

The museums included in Table A8.1 did not develop completely independently. Attention has already been drawn to the influence of Skansen on the development of other museums. Furthermore, the Director of the museum at Arnhem played an important part in developing the original ideas for the Zuiderzee Museum. The first Director of the Black Country Museum (still in post) was previously a member of the Beamish staff and it is unlikely that the similarities between the two museums are purely coincidental. The development of the Welsh Folk and Ulster Folk and Transport Museums were also linked in various ways: see Evans (1988). Common environmental influences were at work among some of the museums: for example, the three Scandinavian museums were opened within 14 years of each other, at a time when the search for national identity and desire to preserve something of the past in the face of growing industrialization was particularly strong. Again, Beamish, the Black Country Museum and Ironbridge – all concerned, to a greater or lesser degree, with industrial history – were established within a fairly short period of each other at a time of rapid industrial change. On the other hand, the initial stimulus for the formation of the Zuiderzee Museum came from a very particular cause: the closure of the Zuiderzee, and the consequent need to provide employment for the local population adversely affected by the building of the dam.

References

Archer, B.H. (1977) *Tourism Multipliers: The State of the Art*, Bangor Occasional Papers in Economics No. 11, Cardiff: University of Wales Press.

Archer, B.H. (1982) 'The Value of Multipliers and Their Policy Implications', *Tourism Management*, **3**, 236–41.

Archer, B.H. (1984) 'Economic Impact: Misleading Multiplier', *Annals of Tourist Research*, **11**, 517–18.

Ashworth, J. and Johnson, P.S. (1990) 'Holiday Tourism Expenditure: Some Preliminary Econometric Results', *Tourist Review*, **3**, 12–18.

Atkinson, F. (1968) 'Regional Museums', *Museums Journal*, **68**, 74–7.

Atkinson, F. (1975) 'Presidential Address', *Museums Journal*, **75**, 103–5.

Atkinson, F. (1985) 'The Unselective Collector', *Museums Journal*, **85**, 9–11.

Barnett, R.R. (1984) *Tourism's Contribution to Employment in York*, Report to York City Council.

Brown, John (1986) *Increasing the Visitor Appeal of the Welsh Folk Museum: Main Report*, prepared for the National Museum of Wales and the Wales Tourist Board: Leigh, Worcestershire.

Darnell, A.C., Johnson, P.S. and Thomas, R.B. (1989) *Modelling Museum Visitor Flows: a Case-Study of the North of England Open Air Museum at Beamish*, Tourism Working Paper No. 4, revised, Durham: Department of Economics, University of Durham (April).

Darnell, A.C., Johnson, P.S. and Thomas, R.B. (1990) 'Modelling Visitor Flows: a Case Study of Beamish Museum', *Tourism Management*, **11**, 251–7.

de Jong, A.A.M. (1988) 'From "Traditional Life" to "Daily Life": Some Impressions from the History of the Netherlands Open Air Museum', lecture given to the 13th Conference of the Association of European Open Air Museums, Ballenberg.

Department of Employment (1986) *Coordination Report: North East Region*, Newcastle: DE (Regional Enterprise Unit).

137

Department of Employment (1987) *Tourism '87: Making the Most of Heritage*, London: DE.

Department of Employment (1989) *Employment News*, No. 173, (February) London.

Evans, E.E. (1988) 'The Early Development of Folklife Studies in Northern Ireland', in Gailey (ed.), pp. 22–3.

Frey, B.S. and Pommerehne, W.W. (1989) *Muses and Markets*, Oxford: Blackwell.

Gailey, A. (1988) *The Use of Tradition. Essays presented to G.B. Thompson*, Cultra, Co. Down: Ulster Folk and Transport Museum.

Grampp. W.G. (1989) *Pricing the Priceless*, New York: Basic Books.

Harris, A.H., Lloyd, M.G., McGuire, A.J. and Newlands, D.A. (1987) 'Incoming Industry and Structural Change: Oil and the Aberdeen Economy', *Scottish Journal of Political Economy*, 34, 69–90.

Henderson, D.M. (1975) *The Economic Impact of Tourism: A Case Study of Greater Tayside*, Edinburgh: Tourism and Recreation Research Unit, Edinburgh University.

Hendon, W.S., Shanahan, J.L., and MacDonald, A.J. (1980) *Economic Policy for the Arts*, Cambridge, Mass.: Abt Books.

Hudson, K. (1987) *Museums of Influence*, Cambridge: Cambridge University Press.

Hughes, G. (1989) 'Measuring the Economic Value of the Arts', *Policy Studies Institute*, 9, 33–45.

Jewkes, J., Sawers, D. and Stillerman, R. (1969) *The Sources of Invention*, 2nd edn, London: Macmillan.

Johnson, P.S. and Ashworth, J.S. (1990) 'Modelling Tourism Demand: a Summary Review', *Leisure Studies*, 9, 145–60.

Johnson, P.S. and Thomas, R.B. (1989a) *Measuring the Local Employment Impact of a Tourist Attraction: An Empirical Study*, Tourism Working Paper No. 6, Durham: Department of Economics, University of Durham (September).

Johnson, P.S. and Thomas, R.B. (1989b) *The Development of Beamish: An Assessment*, Tourism Working Paper No. 3, Durham: Department of Economics, University of Durham (April).

Johnson, P.S. and Thomas, R.B. (1989c) *Working Notes on the Calculations for Tourism, Working Paper No. 6*, mimeo, Durham: Department of Economics, University of Durham (July).

Johnson, P.S. and Thomas, R.B. (1990a) *A Report on a Survey of Visitors to Beamish Museum*, Tourism Working Paper No. 9, Durham: Department of Economics, University of Durham (July).

Johnson, P.S. and Thomas, R.B. (1990b) *Beamish: Some Comparisons*, Tourism Working Paper No. 8, Durham: Department of Economics, University of Durham (June).

Johnson, P.S. and Thomas, R.B. (1990c) 'Employment in Tourism: a Review', *Industrial Relations Journal*, 21, 36–49.

Johnson, P.S. and Thomas, R.B. (1990d) 'Measuring the Local Employment Impact of a Tourist Attraction: an Empirical Study', *Regional Studies*, 24, 395–403.

Johnson, P.S. and Thomas, R.B. (1990e) 'The Development of Beamish: an Assessment', *Museum Management and Curatorship*, 9, 5–24.

Johnson, P.S. and Thomas, R.B. (1990f) 'Tourism in the North: an Employment Profile of the North of England Open Air Museum at Beamish', *Northern Economic Review*, Summer, 25–38.

Johnson, P.S. and Thomas, R.B. (1991a) 'Museums and the Local Economy', in G. Kavanagh (ed.) *The Museums Profession: Internal and External Relations*, Leicester: Leicester University Press.

Johnson, P.S. and Thomas, R.B. (1991b) 'Museums: an Economic Perspective', *New Research in Museum Studies: An International Series*, forthcoming.

Johnson, P.S. and Thomas, R.B. (1991c) 'The Comparative Analysis of Tourist Attractions', in C. Cooper (ed.) *Progress in Tourism, Recreation and Hospitality Management*, London: Frances Pinter, pp. 114–29.

Johnson, P.S. and Thomas, R.B. (1991d) 'The Employment Potential of a Tourist Attraction: a Study of a Museum', *Tourism Studies*, forthcoming.

Longford, J.I. (1972) *The Black Country Museum: Origins and Early Days*, Dudley: The Friends of the Black Country Museum.

MA (1987) *Museums UK. The Findings of the Museums Data-Base Project*, London: Museums Association.

McCrone, G. (1969) *Regional Policy in Britain*, London: Allen & Unwin.

Martin, C.A. and Witt, S.F. (1988) 'Substitute Prices in Models of Tourism Demand', *Annals of Tourism Research*, 15, 255–68.

140   *Tourism, museums and the local economy*

Medlik, S. (1988) *Tourism and Productivity*. Report for the British Tourism Authority and the English Tourist Board, London: BTA/ETB.

Metcalf, H. (1987) *Employment Structures in Tourism and Leisure*, Falmer, Brighton: Institute for Manpower Studies, University of Sussex.

Morgan, J.N. (1986) 'The Impact of Travel Costs on Visits to US National Parks: Intermodal Shifting Among Grand Canyon Visitors', *Journal of Travel Research*, **24** (3), 23–8.

Myerscough, J. (1988) *The Economic Importance of the Arts in Britain*, London: Policy Studies Institute.

Northern Region Strategy Team (1976) *Growth and Structural Change in the Economy of the Northern Region*, Technical Report No. 4, Newcastle: NRST.

Owen, T.M. (1988) 'The Role of a Folk Museum', in Gailey (ed.).

Papadopoulos, S.I. and Witt, S.P. (1985) 'A Marketing Analysis of Foreign Tourism in Greece', in S. Shaw, L. Sparks and E. Kaynak (eds) *Proceedings of the Second World Marketing Congress*, Stirling.

Peacock, A. and Godfrey, C. (1974) 'The Economics of Museums and Galleries', *Museums Journal*, **74**, 55–8.

Peate, I.C. (1971) 'The Welsh Folk Museum', *Glamorgan Historian*, **7**, 161–72.

Pesaran, M.H. and Pesaran, B. (1987) *DATA-Fit. An Interactive Econometric Software Package*, Oxford: Oxford University Press.

Robbins, L. (1963) 'Art and the State', in L. Robbins (ed.) *Politics and Economics*, London: Macmillan.

Rodgers, G. and Rodgers, J. (eds) (1989) *Precarious Jobs in Labour Market Regulation: The Growth of Atypical Employment in Western Europe*, Geneva: International Labour Organisation (International Institute for Labour Studies).

Sinclair, T. and Sutcliffe, C. (1978) 'The First-Round of the Keynesian Regional Income Multiplier', *Scottish Journal of Political Economy*, **25**, 177–86.

Sinclair, T. and Sutcliffe, C. (1982) 'Keynesian Income Multipliers with First and Second Round Effects: an Application to Tourist Expenditure', *Oxford Bulletin of Economics and Statistics*, **44**, 321–38.

Sinclair, T. and Sutcliffe, C. (1987) 'Truncated Income Multipliers and Local Income Generation over Time', *Studies in Economics*, **87/10** (November), Canterbury: University of Kent.

Thiew, T., Wanhill, S. and Westlake, J. (1983), 'Grant Aided Tourism Projects and Employment Creation', *Tourism Management*, **4**, 107–17.

Throsby, C.D. and Withers, G.A. (1979) *The Economics of the Performing Arts*, London: Edward Arnold.

Throsby, C.D. and Withers, G.A (1986) 'Strategic Bias and the Demand for Public Goods', *Journal of Public Economics*, **31**, 307–27.

Valen-Sendstad, F. (1986) *Maihaugen. The Sandvig Collections*, translated by T.D. Edmonston. Lillehammer.

Vaughan, D.R. (1976) *The Economic Impact of the Edinburgh Festival*, Edinburgh: Scottish Tourist Board.

Vaughan, D.R. (1977) *The Economic Impact of Tourism in the Edinburgh and Lothian Region*, Edinburgh: Scottish Tourist Board.

Vaughan, D.R. (1986) *Estimating the Level of Tourism Related Employment: an Assessment of Two Non-Survey Techniques*, prepared by DRV Research for BTA/ETB Research Services, Bournemouth: DRV Research.

Vaughan, D.R. and Long, J. (1982) 'Tourism as a Generator of Employment: a Preliminary Appraisal of the Position in Great Britain', *Journal of Travel Research*, Fall, 27–31.

Wanhill, S.R.C. (1988) 'Tourism Multipliers under Capacity Constraints', *Service Industries Journal*, **8**, 136–42.

Williams, H.E., Joyce, F.E. and Griffin, D.A. (1977) 'The Impact of the National Exhibition Centre on the Local Economy', in F. Joyce (ed.) *Metropolitan Development and Change. The West Midlands: a Policy Review*, Farnborough: Teakfield.

Witt, S.F. (1980) 'An Abstract Mode-Abstract (Destination) Node Model of Foreign Holiday Demand', *Applied Economics*, **12**, 163–80.

Witt, S.F. and Martin, C.A. (1985) 'Forecasting Future Trends in European Tourist Demand', *Tourist Review*, **4**, 12–20.

Witt, S.F. and Martin, C.A. (1987a) 'Econometric Models for Forecasting International Tourism Demand', *Journal of Travel Research*, **25** (3), 23–30.

Witt, S.F. and Martin, C.A. (1987b) 'International Tourism Demand Models – Inclusion of Marketing Variables', *Tourism Management*, March, 33–40.

Index

143

Jewkes, J., Sawers, D. and
Stillerman, R. 88
jobs 50–51, 60–62
Johnson, P. S. and Ashworth, J. S.
81–2
Johnson, P. S. and Thomas, R. B.
5, 10, 12–13, 34, 36, 38, 62, 84,
94–7, 102, 104, 121–2
Joint Committee 18–21, 23–5, 27,
33

key activity 51, 53–4, 58–62, 90–91,
99, 105, 108, 110

labour costs 38–42, 46–8
labour productivity 45–6, 49
Lewis, Peter xii, 3, 31
local authorities 16–35, 61, 100–101
Longford, J. E. 135

Maihaugen 86–8, 96, 101, 129, 132,
136
management, 25–7, 35–6, 42, 81,
89–91, 96, 100
Manpower Services Commission
25, 29, 48
marginal direct tax rate 55
marginal product of labour 49
marginal propensity to consume 55
marginal propensity to import 55,
99, 113
market share 27, 50, 106
marketing 27–8, 66–9, 76, 81–2, 94
Martin, C. A. and Witt, S. F. 82
McCrone, G. 37
Medlik, S. 49
Metcalf, H. 49
Morgan, J. N. 82
multiplier 10, 52, 55–6, 60, 111,
113–14
Museums Association 39
'Museum in the Making' exhibition
20
Museum of the Year Award 12
Myerscough, J. 13, 15, 62, 103–4

national museums 39
net employment 53, 57–62, 108,
115–20

Netherlands Open Air Museum
(Arnhem) 12, 85, 87–8, 96,
101, 129, 132, 136
North of England 6
North Region Strategy Team 114
Norwegian Folk Museum 87–8, 96,
101, 129, 132, 136

objectives 36, 89, 91
off-peak period 94, 123
open air museums 84–9, 129–36
option demand 5, 98
Owen, T. M. 129

Papadopoulos, S. I. and Witt, S. R.
82
party size 81
Peacock, A. and Godfrey, C. 13, 37
peak period 51, 81, 94, 100, 121
Peate, I. C. 135
Pesaran, M. H. and Pesaran, B.
128
price discrimination 95, 97
price elasticity 75, 79–80, 94–5
pricing 21, 33, 70, 84, 93–4
private donations 96–8, 104
product life cycle 36, 84–9
product mix 38
product quality 63–4
productivity of labour 46
public funding of museums 13, 91–
2, 96, 100–104
public policy 100–104

quality dummies 74–5, 78–9
quality of visitor experience 4, 63–
4, 74, 78, 91
queuing 21, 63

reference area 10, 48, 50–51, 53–5,
57–8, 60–62, 99, 100, 118–20
repeat visits 69–70, 76–7, 79–80, 94
research 38–9, 103
retailing 92, 94–6, 102, 109, 135
Robbins, L. 13
Rodgers, G. and Rodgers, J. 61

sales–employment ratio 62, 109